The Push-Pull Marriage

The Push-Pull Marriage

learning and living the art of give-and-take

Les Carter

Baker Book House

Grand Rapids, Michigan 49506

Dedicated with
love and appreciation to
my wife, Shelba Carter,
and to our daughter, Cara

Contents

Preface

We humans tend to be creatures of habit. Once we settle into a routine it's hard for us to break away from the familiar. For example, it is common for most folks to go to bed at about the same time each night, to sit in the same pew each week at church, and to use the same tired phrases in conversations. Did you ever think of your marriage as fitting a consistent pattern? It's true; your style of marital interaction probably falls into a readily identifiable pattern.

Two prominent, recognizable patterns of marriage are explored in this book. One pattern, the push-pull, brings frustration to husbands and wives. It is characterized by subtle (or sometimes not so subtle) "tug-of-war games." When partners find themselves pushing and pulling, they usually find themselves throwing their hands up in frustration and asking, "Why can't we have a more enjoyable marriage?" This is a pattern to be avoided at all costs.

On the other hand, the give-and-take pattern makes positive use of characteristics such as flexibility and optimism. When couples make a concerted effort to work the art of give-and-take into their style of marriage they find companionship and satisfaction. The marital partnership becomes a true pleasure.

It strikes me that the most important human relationship attainable, marriage, is the one which we adults tend to be the least prepared for. Most of us had little training, if any at all, in the fine art of being marital partners. We just learn by the old trial-and-error method. Some couples are fortunate enough to enjoy good results. Others find themselves pushing and pulling. They find themselves in a rut of aggravation.

If you are in the push-pull pattern of marriage, don't despair.

There's hope. Patterns are acquired through practice. This means that as you become aware of the behavior common to each of these two marital patterns, you can choose to weed out the habits that pose problems and incorporate the habits that will result in the satisfying marriage you've always wanted.

Awareness of your patterns is the key to change and progress. As you become conscious of the behaviors that detract from a good marriage, you can concentrate on eliminating them from your interaction style. And as you mentally focus on the actions and attitudes that are intended to bring you closer to a biblically based marriage, you will realize your God-given ability to be the kind of spouse who contributes to a sound, rewarding relationship.

Read the pages of this book with an open mind. Expect to learn something about yourself. You can afford to be hopeful about yourself and your marriage because with an increased awareness of your patterns, you can commit yourself to be more like the spouse God wants you to be.

Introduction

The organ's last powerful strains of "The Wedding March" echoed in the sanctuary. Seconds later I watched the delicate figure in white and the mustached young man standing nervously at her side repeat their vows. Shadowy, subdued light from flickering candles enhanced the beauty of the bride's face. As the vows were completed, I wondered what lay in store for the happy pair.

Would this marriage end in shipwreck on uncertain shores? It was possible. Only time would tell.

Sobering statistics reminded me that one out of every three couples who march to the altar might eventually walk into divorce courts. Marriage, I knew, had a less than perfect track record. Too frequently it was approached with frivolity and left with little regret, despite the abundance of information available on success in marriage.

Years of counseling had introduced me to many couples who had entered into plastic-coated disposable marriages packed in throwaway cartons. Such marriages were designed to self-destruct in a few years or less. And information alone was not the solution.

You may know a lot about marriage. But do you have a good marriage? What do you want out of marriage, and what are you contributing to meet your goals for a successful relationship? And when your marriage seems less than good, what behavior patterns cause this? Why are you and your mate reacting negatively toward each other?

As a marriage partner, be aware of what you are doing and why. This kind of awareness and understanding will close the gap between your information and your actions. It will bring your goals and your actions in line.

The Push-Pull Marriage is written not merely to increase your store of information, but also to increase your happiness level by teaching you to recognize, intercept, and minimize the push-pull patterns within your own marriage. The meaning of the push-pull pattern is explored, its characteristics are discussed, and key factors involved in changing this pattern are given. Once aware of the subtle ways you can entangle yourself, you will feel more capable of putting your store of information into good use and building an exciting marriage.

part one

The Trials of a
Push-and-Pull Marriage

1

Push-Pull: What Is It?

I was only in grade school, but old enough to spot trouble. Aunt Rae was big trouble, and she was headed toward me, arms outstretched. She loomed above me, clasping white-gloved hands in rapture and cooing through her generous smile. I felt her arms surround me and braced myself for the unavoidable kiss. My insides were gravel, and mentally I was pushing Aunt Rae, perfume and all, away as hard as I could. The ordeal ended when she loosened her clinch. I wriggled away from her, and put distance between us as fast as good manners would allow. To me, kissing was definitely "not cool."

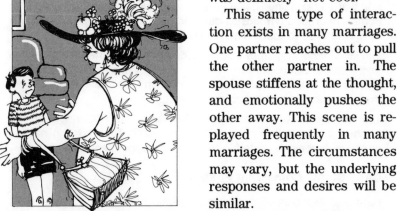

This same type of interaction exists in many marriages. One partner reaches out to pull the other partner in. The spouse stiffens at the thought, and emotionally pushes the other away. This scene is replayed frequently in many marriages. The circumstances may vary, but the underlying responses and desires will be similar.

In a push-pull marriage pattern, two energies are going at the same time but each in a different direction. One partner is in a pulling posture, tugging for more involvement from the spouse. The other maintains a pushing stance, determined to avoid and thrust away involvement and participation. One partner (the puller) wants to talk while the other (the pusher) does not. A wife may enjoy freedom, but her husband needs structure. One may want closeness, and the other likes to be left alone. One may want to talk while the other wants silence. One initiates romance, but the other prefers sleep. One wants to socialize whereas the other wants a quiet evening at home. One wants to discuss religion while the other wants to watch TV. One pulls in and the other pushes away. Look at some examples.

Case Study: Alternate Push-Pull

Ann climbed into bed and reached over to pat Tim affectionately. She felt him cringe and slide closer to the edge of the bed, signaling the continuation of another cold war. Tim was still brooding over their early-evening quarrel. Icicles hung in the air. Ann felt frustrated because her efforts for closeness were being pushed aside by her husband.

Later, Tim told me, "She pressured me as soon as I came home. She handed me the bills that came in the mail and then started badgering me about making plans for the weekend." Tim described his reaction: "The only way I could get her to quit pulling at me was to yell at her. I needed to relax, and Ann wouldn't back off."

Ann tearfully explained her actions: "I really look forward to Tim coming home. I'm around our kids all day, and it's nice to have an adult to talk with. And I like to touch him. I'm an affectionate person."

Tim listed other ways they pushed and pulled each other. "I'm what you might call a serious thinker," he explained. "I like to read books and articles on philosophical subjects. But when I try to talk to Ann about them, she shrugs and leaves me hanging."

Tim felt insulted when Ann pushed him away. Their marriage was enmeshed in a constant push-pull motion. Both Tim and Ann needed direction as they alternated in the roles of pushing and pulling.

Case Study: Consistent Push-Pull

Lynn and Ted created a unique push-pull battleground. It wasn't as noisy as Tim and Ann's. It usually began much too quietly.

Lynn had her own picture of what constituted a good marriage. "I like lots of good times together," she told me. "I like for us to go places—do things together."

Ted felt differently: "Peace and quiet," he said, "that's what makes a good marriage. Live and let live." And to prove his point, he would stay in one end of the house puttering while Lynn did whatever she wanted to do: as long as she stayed in another part of the house.

Lynn was dissatisfied. "I want to talk with Ted, but he's usually disinterested." And it was true. Ted was afraid interaction would lead to confrontation.

Lynn didn't give up easily, however. She added tears and complaining to her repertoire and became generally obnoxious in her efforts to draw Ted into meaningful exchange. She was a persistent puller, and Ted was a staunch pusher.

The Push-Pull Pattern

The push-pull pattern is at the core of most marital problems. Both partners have needs, but their needs differ or conflict. One pushes away intrusion and the other does just the opposite. One prefers to squelch communication while the other labors to create full interaction. The push-pull pattern, with its many variations, emerges at the slightest provocation. And roles can change quickly. One spouse may be strenuously pulling at one point in a disagreement only to push just as hard moments later. The pattern may occur daily in some marriages or only periodically in others.

Become aware of this push-pull pattern and learn how to avoid it. A pattern of constructive give-and-take is far more desirable than destructive push-pull encounters. As we explore the different aspects of the push-pull marriage, keep in mind, first of all, that most people tend to be predominantly either a puller or a pusher. But the roles can switch from time to time. Second, with insight and understanding, partners can learn to acknowledge when they are in this lethal pattern, and they can change. The pushers and the pullers described in this book are not meant to box you into neatly-labeled categories. Rather, they are described to heighten awareness so you can progress.

Look at some of the telltale characteristics that signal a push-pull marriage.

1. Downhill arguing. Patterns of push and pull generally result in angry exchanges. And usually it isn't constructive anger. Hot, angry words can cause deep wounds. Problems may be pointed out but solutions rarely result. Stubbornness rather than flexible communication prevails.

2. Poor listening. Listening skills in a push-pull marriage are usually extremely poor (hearing and listening are not the same).

One person expresses a need but the need doesn't register with the spouse. In this situation, the personal needs of one block out the communicated needs of the other.

3. Game-playing. Each partner wants to come out on top of every power struggle. Games of one-upmanship become the norm, and neither partner is willing to concede, so the struggle goes on.

4. Using control tactics. The kinds of techniques marriage partners use to effectively achieve their goals are limited only by imagination. Some favorite control tactics employed by both pushers and pullers are: shouting, silence, leaving the room, arguing, withholding sex, pleading, procrastinating, or threatening divorce.

5. Playing with truth. Couples enmeshed in a push-pull marriage find it very easy to "play with" truth. They may twist and turn it to suit their purposes, or color it if doing so will give them an advantage. They may not lie directly, but they avoid complete honesty. It's too costly.

6. "My-needs"-are-most-important syndrome. In a push-pull pattern, it becomes easy to focus only on "my needs." Selfishness prevails, creating a feeling of futility and empty desperation. The self-focused partner begins to feel that "If something is not done soon to solve *my* problem, I won't be any good to the marriage anyway."

7. Picking up the "same ol' problems." Push-pull patterns easily develop habitual behavior that produces unsatisfactory resolutions. Root problems that fuel conflicts in the first place get stored on the shelf for future reference. Issues are never really solved. One or both partners eventually feel the urge to come back and pick up the leftover problems. "Maybe this time," they think, "we can resolve it for good." What a waste of energy.

8. Quitting too quickly. Confrontation takes energy. And when push-pull confrontation continues on a regular basis, it's easy to become tired and defeated. Hope withers when no positive change takes place. Good intentions dissolve in feelings of defeat.

Pinpoint Your Position

True, it is hard to break out of a push-pull pattern because humans are creatures of habit. They tend to do what is most familiar, even when they know it is bad for them. If only there was a simple formula for a successful marriage — a pill that could be taken with breakfast. It's not that simple, but learned patterns like this can be broken. Couples who find themselves pushing and pulling one another are not doomed to total misery. There is a way out!

Marriage manuals, seminars, and tapes all have their place, but knowledge must be coupled with understanding because, in the final analysis, understanding is the key to change. Understand both yourself and your spouse.

At this point, you may feel like an Iowa farmer who had just landed at LaGuardia airport for a visit with his sister. He had a letter from her with her address and some instructions but they didn't make any sense to him. Without even knowing what direction her house was from the airport, how could he get there? Finally, he bought a city map, applied his knowledge of map reading, and positioned himself. He was ready to go. He pinpointed his position in relationship to where his sister lived. All that remained was selecting the best route to get there. He now had an overall picture.

This kind of picture is what you need as you begin your pursuit of a better marriage. You will need to determine your present position on the entire landscape of your marriage.

To help you do this, let's examine the components of both pushing and pulling before we look at a give-and-take marriage. Then you will be able to move on optimistically to positive change.

2

Meet the "Pushers"

Case Study: Pusher Husband

Joan brushed the hair out of her eyes and sighed. The headache had plagued her all day, but there was so much to do, and it really had to be done. "I've had headaches for years," she told me. "When we were dating, Eric always seemed so genuinely concerned." It was a different story now. Joan longed for some sympathetic understanding when she had headaches, but it seldom came. Eric consistently pushed Joan's concerns away.

"I bought a business a few years ago," Eric explained. "It takes every bit of energy I can muster to keep it going. It's on my mind constantly." Joan knew this was so, and resorted to crying, nagging, and even shouting to be heard. She was always in pursuit. And he was always defensively pushing her away.

You have probably watched young boys play sandlot football and noticed that a good ball carrier uses one technique to give him an advantage over his would-be tacklers. After tucking the ball close to his side with one arm, he keeps his other arm stiff to fend off any opposing player who approaches him. Those who are adept at using the stiff-arm technique usually are star players.

It doesn't take much insight to recognize that those sandlot youngsters are actually playing more than just football. In reality their games are forerunners of the adult game of one-upmanship.

Married people who communicate by pushing are like

ball carriers who stiff-arm their opponents. When their partner approaches with problems, questions, or simple conversation, they give stiff-armed opposition. Pushers are wary of "trespassers" who invade their turf. They try to run before they are "tackled," and protect themselves by pushing away unwelcome opposition. They push for distance while their spouse pulls for interaction.

Since there are usually two sides to conflicts, pushers are not always wrong. Often pushers have valid thoughts, complaints, and needs when tensions arise. But there is a lot of room for improvement in the way they handle conflict. A gentler, more open style of communication is usually needed.

In most marriages, one partner is much more of a pusher than the other. We all have some of the pusher in us. When a push-pull marriage exists, each mate (even the greatest puller) can sometimes slip into this pattern. Figure 1 lists twenty-five of the most common characteristics found in people who resist interaction by pushing.

If you have ten or more of these traits, you probably have a strong tendency to be a pusher. In most any marriage both partners can move in and out of the pusher traits. Usually one partner pushes more than the other. If both partners have strong pusher tendencies, watch out! Conditions are ripe for plenty of conflict if loving guidelines are not closely followed.

Why Does a Pusher Push?

What causes the pusher style? To answer this question, we will examine six of the most prominent traits of pushers. We need to find out why they "push." Keep in mind that behavior directly reflects an individual's self-image. Ultimately people need to take a good look at their feelings about themselves to understand why they do what they do. You or your spouse may not have all the personal traits mentioned here, but you may find some characteristics that you will want to modify.

Resistant nature. Resistance is a cornerstone in the pusher style of marital interaction. Most adults, at times, resist authority

Figure 1   Pushers

1. Do not like to be disturbed.
2. Like to do things in unvarying patterns.
3. Often resort to power tactics (silent treatment, hard-headed resistance, etc.).
4. Are touchy about being told what to do.
5. Usually have a strong competitive nature.
6. Are perfectionists in some areas.
7. May be described by others as bossy or controlling.
8. Prefer to keep their emotions hidden.
9. Are conscientious and orderly.
10. May be considered by others as stubborn.
11. Tend to be critical.
12. Are strict.
13. Express strong convictions.
14. Express anger easier than warmth.
15. Tend to be self-willed.
16. Complain about feeling smothered.
17. Find that interpersonal relations are stiff.
18. Expect a lot from other people.
19. Give love and acceptance conditionally.
20. Admire the take-charge attitude (as long as no one imposes this on them).
21. Are often preoccupied.
22. Find it difficult to admit mistakes openly.
23. Demand complete loyalty from those closest to them.
24. Cringe at criticism.
25. Are cautious about deeply personal involvements.

figures or controlling agencies. Pushing, in a very real sense is resistance. Pushers are trying to make a statement. They want to be left alone to pursue their personal goals. They don't want anyone to "horn in" on their usual style of doing things. Pushers balk, asserting their need for independence, whenever someone begins to pull them in another direction.

Case Study: Resistant Nature

Jerry's associates would describe him as a friendly fellow. He was easy-going and very ready to engage in pleasant conversation. But at home he exhibited a trait that was well hidden from his social acquaintances.

Jerry had his own set routine and disliked any diversions. His wife could speak to him only at times convenient to Jerry. When problems needed to be discussed she would have to wait until he felt he could spare the time for a distraction. In short, Jerry was a good guy only when he could control his circumstances. He resisted any intrusion into his neatly packaged life.

Pushers may express themselves in a resistant manner but what they have to say is often correct. Their resistance may be legitimate protest and often is their defense against rejection by their spouse.

Demanding nature.   "Keep the counters clean." "Fold the newspaper when you're through." "Try to be on time tomorrow." "Don't interrupt me, I'm watching my favorite program right now."

Remarks like these come from pushers. Many pushers are great demanders but they don't like to take their own medicine from the spouse. That is, they resent others ordering them around. They demand because they have carefully structured their living patterns and don't want them altered. They expect others to follow their chosen patterns. They have strong ideas, and when another person poses a threat, they become demanding. It's one way they can push opposition away.

There are other reasons pushers become demanding: (1) As children, they may have learned to live according to inflexible, predictable patterns, and, as adults, they impose their orderly lifestyle on others. Of course, this means they will be prone to reject any habits of their spouses that differ from their own. (2) Other pushers grew up with more chaos than organization, and compensate by neatly packaging their lives into compartments.

Whatever their background, pushers want and demand conformity, and react strongly when they don't get it. They have little sense of give and take. They are one-sided. The pushers are prone to have a one-track mind, and they don't like anyone disrupting their way of doing things. Complaints from others fall on deaf ears. The pushers feel they are right and avoid attempts from a spouse to communicate openly. They resent any unwanted invasion of their "high" ideals.

Desire to remain uninvolved. Any time people use a pushing technique, they are trying to avoid personal involvement. For example, they may be busy with a project or engrossed in reading a magazine article. If their partner wants to talk, their first instinct is to push the "intruder" away. The partner of a pusher will usually interpret this reaction as close-minded or defensive. Walls of misunderstanding are erected, and mates find themselves farther apart.

Of course, pushers have their own reasons for remaining uninvolved with their mates. Some reasons are understandable; others are inexcusable. These are some of the most popular reasons:

1. Some spouses seem to prefer to be preoccupied. It is difficult to draw them into interaction of any sort, particularly if it is done impatiently and without consideration.

2. When the atmosphere at home gets "hot," some pushers may push their spouse away simply as a protective measure. If they didn't, they would be overwhelmed in one way or another.

3. Most people like to stay with what feels comfortable. They pursue what's familiar to them rather than take risks. Because of this, pushers who lack confidence in their abilities to interact will resist efforts on the part of a spouse to "draw them out."

4. Who enjoys being hurt over and over again? If they have been hurt before, pushers don't want it to happen again. If exposure and interaction were unpleasant before, why risk them again? Arm's length, to the pusher, is a much safer distance.

5. Sometimes it's just a lot easier to please self. Relationships take too much effort to develop. A pusher may not be motivated to exert the needed effort required to fully explore and nourish a relationship with a spouse.

Lazy emotions. Pushers are often reluctant to deal with the "nitty-gritty" of personal relationships. In this sense, they are emotionally lazy. They prefer the path of least resistance. At the same time, most confirmed pushers can be very precise in the nonemotional realm. They are headstrong and pursue tasks doggedly. You might assume that one who would work so hard in task fulfillment would also be adept at handling emotions. Yet, what works for a pusher in task fulfillment can work against him/her in interpersonal relations.

Case Study: A Confirmed Pusher with Lazy Emotions

Jim loved to organize. He organized everything and tolerated little de-
viation from his plans. Karen often attempted to change little things
like mealtimes, but would end up in tears each time. Tears carried no
weight with Jim. He considered her requests a nuisance and a bother.
"Why waste time talking about *why* we should change when we have
it all neatly arranged now?" Jim reasoned. "It's settled."

Emotional laziness may manifest itself when a husband is working on a hobby in the garage and doesn't want to be bothered with
"little problems." Or, maybe a wife is engrossed in a sewing project
and her husband's questions "get in her way." Whenever emotional
laziness is being exercised, the pushers have tunnel vision. They
see only their goal. They become obsessed in pursuing their goals
and seldom make time to deal with emotion-laden issues.

A performance self-image.   Pushers feel fine about themselves and their lives when their environment is in predictable
order. If they can create a neatly-packaged life they have a positive
self-image. If not, their self-image crumbles. A pusher will tend to
work hard to have all the external signs of success. One such sign
is a controlled environment. It represents stability. Other signs are
high achievement at work, being a "perfect" housekeeper, or simply creating a quiet home atmosphere. Pushers don't want to be
bothered with the inconvenient parts of a marriage relationship
because such disarrangement of their controlled environment
threatens their self-image.

A self-image based mostly on orderly external performances
and circumstances is dangerous because there is no such thing as
a perfect performer, and very few ideal circumstances exist. A
pusher knows this intellectually. Even the most diehard pushers
will admit that perfection is beyond their reach. But they continue
to live as if perfection could be achieved. Consequently they set
themselves up for great disappointment and anger.

Americans tend to classify people winners or losers based on
the outward show of success. And pushers have accepted this
standard for themselves and their families. They assume their mar-

riage is good only when everything looks calm on the surface and everyone functions like they are "supposed" to.

A "pulling" spouse. Pushing behavior is often caused by a pulling spouse who refuses to let go. Continual pulling by one partner produces the very reaction most disliked in their mate.

"I don't really try to keep my wife at arm's length," one man told me. "But she is always so intrusive and insistent I don't know if I have a choice." Wives have complained of the same invasion into their lives, which seemed to force them to push their mate away. Obviously the mate of a chronic pusher needs to interact with sensitivity. Pushers often accuse their mate of nagging or being bossy (which may or may not be the case). They are afraid of being overwhelmed by too many requests, too much small talk, or too much criticism. Instinctively they feel the need to throw up a defense mechanism to keep the other "off their turf." They erect barriers to ward off any real or perceived dominance by a spouse.

Pushing patterns can be changed — there is hope. Both spouses need to understand what they're doing when they put this pattern into motion. The pushing partner needs to ask: "What characteristics do I have that cause me to go into my pushing behaviors?" The other partner can ask: "What am I doing to perpetuate my mate's problem?" Chances are that when one partner is frequently pushing, you will probably find a spouse who is pulling. And that leads us to the "puller," which we will discuss in the next section.

3

Meet the "Pullers"

The gate snapped open and a calf ran headlong into the arena with a cowboy in hot pursuit. His lasso whirled rhythmically above his head, his eyes glued to the bawling calf. Suddenly the cowboy released his rope, which dropped snakelike around the calf's neck. A split second later the taunt rope flipped the calf to the ground in a cloud of dust. The cowboy dismounted, sprang to the calf's side, and deftly twisted a shorter rope around the calf's legs. His raised arms signaled victory and ignited a deafening roar from the rodeo crowd.

A lot of marriages resemble a calf-roping contest. One partner (the puller) is chasing, while the spouse (the pusher) seeks escape from the "rope" that threatens freedom or privacy. Pullers don't give up easily either. Sometimes their efforts are obvious, like the calf roper; at other times they are subtle. Subtle or not, they are out to pull their partner in — by persuasion and coercion.

Pullers like to talk things over. They want to get feelings and ideas out in the open. They seek answers to their questions. They want closeness and predictability. When gaps open up in the relationship they move immediately to close them. Their efforts often come across as insistent, selfish, or overemotional. They crave closeness, and when they don't find it they feel the need to pull the hesitant spouse over to their way of thinking.

The pullers' desire for closeness does not automatically make them neurotic. Not at all. All people need the sense of security and contentment that comes from love or companionship with someone else. Most people want to be close to someone. You want to feel liked. You want the assurance that others, especially your mate, thinks you are okay. This is a natural, God-given instinct that draws people toward others.

Pullers run into trouble, however, because they exaggerate their normal need for closeness, and begin to communicate in a style that actually works against them rather than for them. They try to force closeness from their mates if they can't get it any other way. A spouse's resistance to closeness may be wrong, but the pullers only add to the problem by trying to force closeness upon a stubborn partner. In their eagerness, they foster resentment.

We all tend to pull our partners sometimes, but one partner usually does it more than the other. This perpetuates the push-pull pattern, because when one partner pulls too strongly, the other usually reacts by pushing.

Case Study: The Puller

"Hello, honey, do you like my new hairstyle? Should I wear this dress tonight or change to my green suit? Let's eat out, I feel like celebrating." This was Elsie's nonstop greeting.

Lance answered the first two questions with a grunt and the last one with a decided, "No."

Immediate gloom settled over Elsie. She was angry and began banging pots and slamming cupboard doors. "He didn't even give me a hug. Neither did he look at my new hairstyle. It's no use trying to look attractive. I'm just a plain Jane who always looks mousey. Our marriage isn't fun anymore." A couple of tears spilled onto her cheeks.

Lance had retreated behind the paper again. "Whew! that Elsie breezes in here like a whirlwind full of talk. I'm ready for some peace and quiet but it doesn't look like I'm going to get it."

Lance reacted predictably to Elsie's classic pulling attempts by figuratively pushing her out of his quiet, comfortable corner. He thoroughly resented her noisy intrusion. Each partner is putting a high priority on "my feelings."

Figure 2 lists characteristics found in people who tend to pull frequently.

Figure 2 **Pullers**

1. Often let emotions rule them. They are feeling-oriented.
2. Spontaneously enjoy the fun things in life.
3. Sometimes speak before they think.
4. Need outward evidences of being loved.
5. Allow emotions to fluctuate.
6. Rely on the approval of others for self-esteem.
7. Have a hard time delaying gratification.
8. Would be described by others as sensitive.
9. Find their emotions easily swinging between love and anger.
10. Are capable of thinking logically, but don't always apply it.
11. Sometimes give with the ulterior motive of ultimately "getting."
12. Get angry when they don't get their way.
13. Are skilled at "turning on the charm."
14. Frequently express mood changes.
15. View an unfriendly person as a threat.
16. Like to talk.
17. Described by others as insistent.
18. Like to be with people.
19. Cling to the past.
20. Idealize marriage.
21. Are easily excitable.
22. Can be romantic at times.
23. Sometimes act childlike.
24. Use the word *should* a lot.

Some of these characteristics will pertain to you. Others will not. Notice that most of the characteristics can be either normal or abnormal, depending on the style in which they are exhibited. If you can identify with ten or more of these traits you probably find yourself frequently in the pulling position.

To get an even better picture, let's look specifically at a puller's key personality traits. As was true with the pusher traits, the descriptions may not fit you in all respects. But you may discover some areas that need attention.

A dependent nature. Individuals who are dependent rely on the words and actions of others for emotional stability. When other people are in a good mood, they are in a good mood. But when others are "sour," they, too, take on negative moods. Their emotions depend too much on their circumstances, and this is risky because other people are unpredictable. This explains why pullers try to draw their mates into their way of thinking and behaving. They are afraid that if their needs are not met by the spouse, then marital happiness and contentment will be lost. The happiness of one depends too heavily on the response of the other. Pullers are reactors who hope to control the actions of their mate so they won't have anything negative to react to.

How does a dependent nature develop? Pullers usually come from one of two types of family environments: (1) Their family may have been consistently predictable and reliable. They knew that they could count on someone to "pinch hit" for them when a problem arose. They had their struggles, but they learned very early that when struggles came along, they could look to someone else to make things all right. (2) Their families may have been unemotional and inexpressive. They felt a void in meaningful relationships then, and now they crave positive "strokes." Some people grew up in backgrounds where love and emotions were difficult to express. Not all people respond alike, but persons from such a background often think they are going to make things different now. Their intentions may be solid gold, but often they overcompensate in attempting to create a warm atmosphere before the partner is ready. They may seem to be imposing when actually they are very needy.

Tender feelings. Pullers don't hide their feelings very well. The tone of their voice is frequently emotional and they readily admit to a yearning for emotional involvement. Because they freely expose their emotions, they often wind up feeling hurt and disappointed when things go wrong. They are vulnerable and prone to letdowns.

Pullers are often pegged as being more emotional than logical. Sometimes this may seem to be so, but it does not mean that they are incapable of rational thinking. When they do apply rational thinking to their problems, they discover that they can have more control over their hurts. A wife may convince herself that she can't possibly be happy until her husband changes. But when she thinks about this more rationally, she may recognize that although she is uncomfortable when her husband disappoints her, it is not the end of the world. The same is true for husbands, of course. A person can learn to have more inner control rather than looking to outer sources to make him/her feel better.

Insistent nature. Pullers can be very insistent. After all, they want their way! On the surface, their insistence resembles the demands of the pusher. But looking deeper we find the puller's attitude is different. The demanding pusher tries to create a gap, whereas the insistent puller wants to force a showdown. Here. Now. Together.

Pullers waste no words explaining what the spouse is supposed to be doing. "Don't you know that when mother visits you should give her the best chair?" Or, "Surely you remember that you are supposed to talk with me before you go on a spending spree."

Very often, pullers have legitimate requests to express. True, a mate may need to be reminded of wrong-doing or neglect. But insistent pullers are often unaware of how offensive they can be. Without realizing it, they can cause behaviors opposite from the ones they look for in their partners. In their efforts to be assertive and expressive, they unwittingly put the other person in a defensive posture. And who likes to be backed into a corner? Pullers become overzealous in their pursuit of personal needs.

The urge to control. Pullers are afraid to "live and let live." I have heard pullers proclaim: "I'd like to stop being so insistent, but I'm afraid if I do I won't get any respect." They think they can "create" the kind of partner they need, so instead of taking chances, they begin to control their spouse.

Pullers persistently try to get their partner "back on the track." Diversity, to them, may indicate a mismatch. "Why can't we learn to do the same things and enjoy the same activities?" they ask. Pullers feel more secure when their spouses are more like they are. Such a spouse is more predictable and requires less control.

The controlling nature of pullers usually differs from that of pushers. Pushers tend to seek control of external items while the pullers seek control of internal matters. For example, pushers will want to stick to schedules (external) while pullers will be worried that others will think less of them (internal). Pullers want to control emotions. They don't like their partners to be angry, worried, or indifferent. Ironically, in their efforts to control the feelings of the mate, pullers are prone to let their own feelings get out of hand.

Self-image based on approval of others.   Pullers "like" themselves when they feel others approve of them. Of course, this places a positive self-image on a shaky foundation because there are no guarantees that others will view them positively. A puller married to a supportive mate will maintain a good level of self-esteem. And, of course, the reverse is true: little support from a mate results in low self-esteem.

Many pullers don't realize how they tend to put themselves down when others disapprove of them. They have subconsciously convinced themselves that they are okay only because enough other people tell them they are okay. Their self-image is determined by feedback from other people. Their self-esteem lacks objectivity. Most pullers can recite reasons why an individual is supposed to have positive self-regard. They may admit, for example, that since they are God's children, their worth cannot be threatened by other human beings. But when it comes to internalizing such concepts into a meaningful set of personal guidelines, they fail to do it. More than knowledge, they need insight into how they let themselves be controlled by the opinions of others.

Because they are feeling-oriented, pullers can't perceive their self-image as something they must decide to believe in. Rather, they allow their self-image to bloom only in response to the adoration and respect given to them by others. This kind of dependence causes them to manipulate their mates to receive the support they crave. They actually wind up sabotaging the possibilities for being loved because their actions create friction rather than harmony.

A pushing environment.   In family settings we all affect each other to some degree. For example, if a husband continually keeps his wife at arm's length, the wife will begin to crave something from the pushing husband. It's a natural reaction. If you are married to a partner who seems to pull you in continually, you might ask yourself what you are doing to feed the problem. What need of your spouse are you overlooking?

Pullers often tell me their mates are aloof, distant, or tempermental. "I feel like I'm in their way all the time." They feel unloved and frequently complain that their partner seems afraid of interpersonal involvement. Pullers often sense that their partners don't want to become vulnerable by exposing their inner feelings. In this sense, the puller's spouse may have some insecurities that could use a lot of attention.

Consequently, a successful marriage requires constructive effort by both spouses. When the effort is too one-sided, the chances for harmony decrease markedly. With this in mind, let's take a closer look in the next chapter at the perpetrators of the push-pull pattern. By deepening our understanding, we can open the door to long-range improvement.

4

Push-Pull Technicians: What Makes Them Tick?

Case Study: A Manipulative Puller

Jay, an earnest Christian father, was committed to building a good home. In fact, he was so strongly committed that he launched himself on an all-out self-improvement kick to prove his good intentions. In the process he became perfectionistic, insistent, smug, and exerted strong "pulling" tactics on his wife, Kim. "I expected Kim to be excited about the changes I was making," Jay told me, "but she seems to resist my efforts."

Jay's overtures were not entirely unnoticed or unappreciated. However, he used techniques that negated a lot of his good intentions. He became very adept at laying guilt trips on Kim with remarks such as "Who's the head of this family anyway?" Then Kim would resort to pushing techniques of her own.

Manipulative Push-Pull Techniques

Like Jay and Kim, many couples find themselves entrenched in manipulative push-pull techniques. The strategies are used over and over again in varying situations to accomplish underlying goals. Each wants his/her own way. Married couples who engage in such methods can quickly become sparring partners who "polish" their push-pull techniques on each other to the detriment of the marriage. Neither partner is the winner.

Both pushers and pullers resort to learned techniques, but in different ways. Jay was a puller who wanted more interaction from his wife. He used demands to help reach that goal. Kim wanted to keep Jay at a safe distance and used her own bag of practiced techniques to do it. The maneuvers used by both Jay and Kim worked only on a short-term basis. In the long run, they did little or nothing to cement their marriage.

Push-pull technicians can use on their spouses an endless variety of highly developed strategies which lead to further frustration and difficulty. Let's look at some maneuvers of habitual push-pull "technicians," otherwise known as husbands and wives.

Demands. Both pushers and pullers can resort to demanding techniques. Pullers use demands when other, more gentle or subtle tactics fail to "bring their spouse around." Pushers utilize demands to fend off trespassers on their territory.

Figure 3 **Push-Pull Techniques**

Technique	Used Most By Pusher	Used Most By Puller	Used By Both Pusher and Puller
Demands			X
Guilt trips		X	
Silent treatment			X
Tuning out	X		
Helplessness		X	
Strong opinions	X		
Pleading		X	
Being extra nice		X	
Exaggerating			X
Asking loaded questions			X
Being vague	X		
Using sarcasm	X		
Doing a sales job		X	
Seducing		X	
Making half-hearted efforts	X		
Making threats			X
Pouting			X
Being unreliable	X		
Workaholism	X		

Guilt trips. Pullers are skilled when it comes to persuasion via the guilt trip. Remember Jay? One of his favorite barbs was: "This family would be different if I had some support around here." And Kim would push him with a retort like, "If you knew how to lead better I wouldn't have any trouble following." Verbal clashes like this can easily become a battleground with each one trying to wound the other to prove a point and gain control.

"Well, Wonder Woman, let's see some of your fancy strategy here."

Sad looks are an effective guilt-inducer. Tears will gain attention if not outright support. Another variation is shouting, which can cause a passive partner to cringe in guilt. "I don't believe you would buy that without checking with me first!" Or try this one on for size: "Do you suppose you could help me move this refrigerator, or doesn't it make any difference that I'm seven months pregnant?"

Whatever method is employed, it is an effort to force a partner into another way of thinking. And it's a form of persuasion with a sting in it.

The silent treatment. The silent treatment is a most effective device for interrupting the flow of conversation. On the surface, the silent treatment is a pushing technique to keep pullers at a distance. Pullers, however, also will use this technique to manipulate their spouses. If pullers have needs pushed away by their spouses, they may employ silence as a weapon to either punish their mates or prove their points. When the silent treatment is utilized by both the husband and wife, stubbornness becomes an endurance marathon until one mate gives in. But the victory is only shallow with no real winner.

Tuning out. Tuning out is a polite variation of the silent treatment, but it has less blatant, more subtle manipulative intentions. The spouse doing the tuning out still wants the "invader" to think he or she is listening. Tuning out is deceptive: the body is present but the mind is not. It's an effective pushing tool to keep spouses at a distance and under the delusion that they are being heard.

Helplessness.   Some pullers abuse the word *can't.* It's a helpless technique guaranteed to bring some kind of response. "I need your company tonight; I just can't stand to be alone." Or, "I can't do this by myself" (I really can but would rather not). Although requests for help or companionship can be legitimate, a puller may use the helpless routine as a device to gain the partner's attention.

Strong opinions.   People who voice strong, inflexible opinions may have honest convictions, but some of these self-assured ones (usually pushers) use their rigid opinions to erect a wall around them that few dare to scale or challenge for fear of being put down. Ideas asserted dogmatically leave little room for open communication. Being opinionated is a sure way to keep others at a distance. This is what pushers want. They avoid open exchanges of thoughts and feelings because they might get pulled into a trap that would topple their opinions. Even when their opinions fail the test of logic, they hang on to them. They care less about being right than about staying on top.

Pleading.   The pleading technique is one of the standard behaviors of pullers. Diehard pleaders can be very persuasive and convincing. They don't give up easily. Pleaders, like a dripping faucet, become so tiresome they can't be ignored. Sometimes pleaders will "make a bargain." They are convinced that they must have their way, and they do not ease up until they are satisfied.

Being extra nice.   Being extra nice can be nothing more than a thinly disguised move designed to get one's way. It can work so well that it doesn't even seem to be manipulative. Smiles and grins are a powerful means of controlling the atmosphere, thereby getting needs met. And niceness of this sort is distinctively "pulling" in nature. After all, who can resist all that bubbly charm? "Niceness" will break down a pusher's stubbornness nearly every time.

Exaggerating.   Exaggeration is used by both pushers and pullers, depending on the need. Pullers may exaggerate their needs to convince their spouses to "come over to my side." They make problems into impossible mountains. Complaints are blown all out of proportion. Pullers can paint rainbows all over tasks they want to "share." Exaggeration comes easily to the puller, and often this technique works.

Pushers, on the other hand, use exaggeration to avoid their mates. "I *can't* miss this meeting. It would mean my head." When they describe a headache, it will be so debilitating that they "can't *possibly* be expected to wash the car today." Pushers don't want to be dominated and find exaggeration useful to gain the space they need.

Asking loaded questions.   Both pushers and pullers are afraid to be direct because it means risking an answer they don't want to hear. This fear is the breeding ground for the charade of the loaded question. A pulling spouse is most likely to masquerade behind loaded questions such as: "Would you be nice enough to go get me the hammer?" Or: "I think a real Christian husband would want to take his wife out on a date, don't you?" Here's another: "I can't think of anything more fun than spending an evening together, can you?" A "no" answer means the spouse is obviously an ogre or an uncaring grouch. Loaded questions are traps that demand one obvious answer.

Being vague.   Have you ever known people who talk a lot and sound important, but say virtually nothing at all? They specialize in vague generalities. We often think of politicians as those who erect invisible walls of generalities and double-talk between themselves and others. Husbands and wives too can be experts at this.

Hazy communicators are usually pushers who want to closet their real thoughts and notions. They are reluctant to honestly verbalize their feelings because they might be put down or discredited. Vagueness is a skillful way of pushing intruders outside.

Using sarcasm.   Sarcasm is a weapon used mostly by pushers. The verbal zingers that one spouse throws at the other are intended to keep that person "in place." Sarcasm says "I'm dissatisfied, and I want to make you uncomfortable because it's your fault. Then you'll see things my way." Pullers do a good job of using sarcasm too. They merely dress guilt in a different costume with remarks like, "I suppose you don't have time to help me." If the pullers can cause their mates to feel foolish, they might relinquish their point of view and finally see things the "right" way.

Doing a sales job. Salespeople have one basic objective: to sell their product. A type of sales atmosphere prevails in some discussions between couples. Spouses draw on a surprising array of sales "pitches" in an attempt to meet personal objectives. "That dress is the only one left, it's my best color, it's been reduced three times, and you get paid tomorrow!" Husbands and wives can assume a parent/child posture when it comes to requests such as: "Honey, the guys are going hunting in Colorado for a week . . ." and on it goes. In this sense, the sales job is done from a puller's position. Pullers possess a strong, almost desperate, desire to bring their spouses around to their way of thinking.

Seducing. Seduction is used by pullers who hunger for attention from a partner, and both men and women get into the act. Mates know that if they can turn a spouse's attention to something pleasurable, it will be easier to get the spouse to give in to demands. Seduction can be other than sexual. Husbands like to seduce their wives with fine jewelry or perhaps a night on the town. Wives can cleverly seduce their husbands with a favorite meal or simply with sugar-coated flattery. Seduction can be used in a number of ways: all of them aimed at "getting my way."

Making halfhearted efforts. Some pushers can't seem to say what they think. They feel rebellious and intruded on, but they don't have sufficient confidence to speak out. Avoiding open confrontation, they may become passively aggressive. This is where halfhearted efforts enter in. Their spouse may ask: "Would you mind picking up the dry cleaning on your way home?" Or, "Can you get Mom at the airport?" Whatever task is requested, pushers feel resentment but don't vocalize it. They may go ahead and perform the task but their faces and/or attitudes reveal the displeasure of being imposed on.

Aggravation is indirectly expressed, but the spouse knows it is there. The message is clear: "Okay, but don't bother me like this again."

Making threats. The threatening technique is used frequently from both the push and the pull positions. Pushers use threats in trying to stop their spouses from being insistent: "If you don't quit nagging me, I'll leave and go where no one can find me." Pullers use threats as a desperate attempt to get their way: "If you don't show me any appreciation you can stop counting on hot meals around here!" When couples exchange heated threats, the tension level runs dangerously high. Only an immediate change in the communication style of each partner will neutralize this destructive hostility.

Pouting. An old-fashioned pout can be surprisingly successful and is utilized by both pushers and pullers. Pullers use it when they have tried other methods without success. They feel ignored and assume that if they can put on a sad show they might coerce their spouses to give in to their demands. Pushers pout when they want to keep the walls up high to prevent unwanted intrusions. If a long, sad face can show convincingly that feelings are deeply hurt, maybe the partner will back away.

Being unreliable. When a job is to be done, some people just cannot be counted on to do it. It's not that they are incapable of helping: they simply refuse to try. These unreliable people are pushers saying, "I don't want to get involved." They are really avoiding interaction with someone. By acting unreliably, they feel they will have a better chance of being left alone. It is all a part of the pusher's scheme to live life with the least amount of disruption.

Workaholism. If you're looking for a proven way to put distance between you and your spouse, become a workaholic. Working every available minute is a plausible alibi guaranteed to keep your spouse at a distance. Workaholism is a pushing technique. Most workaholics are uncomfortable with emotions and personal issues. They want to control their own lives totally and keep out-side interference at a minimum. Workaholics are usually great excuse-makers. They claim that their work just has to be done, and to leave it undone would be disastrous. But the truth is that they are either afraid of personal involvement or they lack the courage to work through unresolved anger toward their partners.

Evaluating Your "Techniques"

As you consider your use of the various techniques involved in the push-pull style of interaction, keep this thought in mind. The maneuvers mentioned in this chapter are learned. Once acquired, they are fine tuned by repeated use. But there is hope: what is learned can be changed. New, positive traits can be mastered and substituted for the destructive techniques of the push-pull games.

Is yours a push-pull marriage? Are you interested in changing your situation? You don't have to endure these marriage "hurts" indefinitely. You don't have to put the same old medicine on re-lational sore spots and wonder why healing fails to take place. To improve your situation, step back and ask yourself a couple of questions: What am I honestly trying to accomplish in my mar-riage? Is there a gap between the relationship I want and the relationship I now have? If there is, you need to rethink your goals and decide to engage in fresh actions that will bring about mean-ingful change.

An enjoyable marriage is within the reach of most couples who are willing to change their stressful, push-pull patterns and move toward give-and-take patterns.

The next chapter examines attitudes that will generate new, successful behaviors.

5

Who, Me? Change?

Case Study: Other-oriented Problem Solving

Brenda and Dan told me they had been enmeshed in a push-pull marriage for years. They were like two wrestlers in a match that never ended. And there weren't any cheerleaders on the sidelines. Dan frequently was angry or moody, and his attitudes frightened Brenda. "I don't dare tell him how much his anger hurts me except when he's calm." Sometimes Dan would listen to Brenda, but other times his temper would flare. Brenda would back off.

She desperately tried to change Dan. She taped appropriate Bible verses to the mirror. She often called him at work with a cheery "Have a good day." However, her basic problem was that she did not accept Dan as he was. When she realized this, she began to release her "hold" on him. "As a result," she told me, "Dan began to relax and be himself. As I did my part to create an environment of acceptance, he began to change."

Trying to change someone takes a lot of energy. But some couples work at it tirelessly. When they "hit the mat," they get right back up and try the same old "holds" that failed before. Each one clings to the hope that the other will change. Brenda spent most of her creative energies trying to change Dan. But he didn't change until she changed. She realized her insistence was compounding the tension. She and Dan were involved in "other-oriented" problem solving, which seldom works. It only escalates tensions and resentments. Changes made are usually superficial and temporary. Almost everyone resents having to change at someone else's command.

Other-oriented problem solving has been built into our way of life, however, and it's hard to ignore. We all have little conven-

iences programed into our
lives: conveniences like aspi-
rin, fast-food restaurants, and
newspapers delivered to our
door. In themselves, these
conveniences are innocent
enough. But as a pattern they
train us to look to others for
solutions, and we fail to tap
our own resources. Instead of
learning to cope with struggle

as people did a few generations ago, we detour around struggle in
search of the "quick fix." This attitude spills over into marriage;
couples continue to look to someone or something else for "cure-
alls." It's so much easier to ask a spouse, "What are *you* going to
do about it?" But to have an enjoyable give-and-take marriage, the
focus has to move from "Why don't you change?" to "How can I
change?" Here are five key attitudes to keep in mind as you and
your mate work toward a more satisfying marriage relationship.

1. You can count on me. Husbands and wives are expert at
pointing the finger of guilt away from themselves. When an argument erupts, each partner uses "you" more than any other word
("You never ... Why don't you ... If you would only ..."). Even
when spouses don't say the word *you*, they probably think it. Each
is so preoccupied with the faults of the other that only tentative
moves are made toward any real personal change. Instead, each
partner finds it easier to make a token effort, and then wait for
the spouse to "get on with the program." If there is no reciprocal
move on the part of the spouse, it's easy to quit.

As you try to break this push-pull pattern in your marriage,
begin to develop an attitude that says, "You can count on me."
Solve your own problems before focusing on the problems of your
mate. Determine to improve yourself despite any unpleasant reaction from your mate. You may have setbacks and, at times, slip
back into your old style. But keep picking yourself up — don't quit!
Turn your stubbornness into persistence. Don't let anyone hinder
your efforts to be a better mate.

This attitude will accomplish two things: (1) You will like yourself better because you know you are really trying to be the best person you can. (2) You can influence your spouse in a powerful way. Your efforts to create a more pleasant atmosphere for your mate can be a real incentive for reciprocating support. As you work to create a progressive motion in your marriage, your spouse will find your efforts appealing and your personality increasingly attractive.

2. You are free to be yourself. A major tension in a push-pull marriage is that neither partner feels sufficiently accepted by the other. The efforts and counter-efforts to change each other are recycled continually. The key problem with all these strenuous efforts is that they don't work. The best way to influence your mate toward change is to allow your mate freedom to be his/her own person. You may ask: "If I draw back and offer freedom, won't that backfire on me?" It may. But how successful have your past efforts been? Has forcing change brought about any permanent, positive transformation? Actually, you are not responsible for changing your partner. Your partner is the only one who can initiate personal change.

Freedom is essential to a growing marriage. It is your gift to your mate. Give freedom, and you convey trust and acceptance. You communicate that you are not threatened by differentness. You indicate that you have the maturity to work with what lies ahead. Conversely, when you withdraw freedom (becoming demanding or condemning) you express a lack of trust not only in your spouse but in yourself! You are admitting that your spouse is incapable of positive change. You also communicate a lack of confidence in your own ability to be loving in less than perfect conditions.

Freedom and acceptance go hand in hand. (Note: when you accept someone you don't necessarily condone everything they say and do.) Freedom implies confidence and hope. It is attractive and appealing. By giving other people the "permission" to be who they are, you will help create their receptiveness of you. You will discover that your influence over others actually increases.

You may think giving freedom to your spouse is risky. A wife may say, "If I let my husband do his own thing we'll never get close." Likewise, husbands are afraid to "release" their wives. "Who knows what might happen," some men tell me. "She might never change." So rather than take the risk, both husbands and wives blindly follow old patterns that have failed for years.

There is a paradox at work when you give others the freedom to be who they want to be. The very act of freeing your mate creates an atmosphere free of rebellion or resentment. In this kind of climate, your mate will be motivated to be open and honest with you. Your desires will be taken more seriously because your spouse will not feel defensive or tied down. Consequently, there will be room for mature exchange. Both of you will be open-minded. Nourished by freedom, communication flourishes. Deprived of freedom, communication grows crooked and becomes manipulative.

3. I'll consider your needs. As soon as you do a good turn, do you begin to watch for "the payback?" Marriage partners often fall prey to this kind of thinking, and it inevitably leads to a push-pull pattern. Sooner or later, one partner is going to become insistent or complaining. Each partner comes to expect an ulterior motive behind every kindness.

When you give expecting something in return, you may sabotage chances for a consistent pattern of loving. Couples do much better in their improvement efforts when each partner works at meeting the needs of the other without expecting something in return. Giving has its own built-in rewards. Even when you don't get instant results, you can feel comfortable with yourself because you are genuinely trying to be a part of the solution. Someone needs to take the initiative to be understanding and responsive. It might as well be you! The "pay off" may take a while, but even while you are waiting you are winning.

4. It may not be fair, but I'll keep working. "It seems like I'm doing all the work at improving our marriage." I frequently hear this in counseling sessions. "It's not fair," they tell me. And I have to agree. It isn't fair for one person to work harder than the other. But when we stop to consider the alternatives, we find that fairness is not really the issue. And even though it's unfair for one to do all or most of the work, it is better than neither one making any effort at all.

Case Study: One-sided Effort

Cheryl had been married for eleven years and had a six-year-old son. Cheryl's husband seemed to be totally turned off by tenderness. He was rarely sensitive to Cheryl and spent little time with their son. "When I try to be loving he's gruff in return," she told me. Naturally, her feelings were hurt. She began having frequent bouts with loneliness, anger, and depression. When she came to my office she would cry, "It's not fair! I try so hard to be a good wife, but look where it gets me. Nowhere!" But then we looked at her alternatives. Cheryl had been through one divorce, and she desperately wanted to avoid another. So that option was out. She could choose to stay depressed, but that wasn't very appealing either. She could yell at her husband, but she knew where that would lead. Considering her alternatives, Cheryl decided that although it wasn't necessarily fair, she could be happier with herself if she would continue to make an effort to be a loving wife.

When you decide to improve your marriage ask yourself, "What is most profitable?" It may not seem fair for you to work harder than your spouse, but it may be the best possible solution. You have a choice in the way you handle yourself. You can choose to let your circumstances dictate the way you behave or you can choose to get control of your lifestyle in spite of an imperfect family situation. This takes much personal initiative, but the rewards are worth it.

5. We are going to improve. As a final thought, you may be aware that some people make all the "right" efforts to put their marriage on the right track. But beneath the surface they're deeply skeptical. They think: "Okay, I'll give it a try, but I'll be shocked if anything changes." This kind of attitude virtually guarantees failure.

Efforts at improvement must be combined with a positive attitude that expects results. Positive attitudes applied to adverse circumstances can make things happen! But don't expect changes overnight. Nor should you expect to achieve perfection. You can, however, look forward to definite improvement in your overall pattern.

By taking a positive attitude, notice how you are affirming the notion that you are a capable person. You are saying "yes" to your part in improving your marriage. You are recognizing your contribution as significant. You know that your behaviors and attitudes will make a difference.

At the same time, be realistic. Expect positive results, but don't be blinded to the reality that the road toward a successful marriage requires a lot of work. Improvement may require determined, strenuous effort and discipline on your part. And you may get some injuries in the process.

But your goal is well worth the required energy to reach it. A healthy marriage is satisfying and nourishing to each partner. Keep that goal in mind—it will see you through temporary setbacks and fuel your energies for further progress ahead.

part two

The Joy of a Give-and-Take Marriage

6

Give-and-Take: What's It All About?

To some, give-and-take marriage means simply "I'll take everything my partner wants to give me." But a bona fide give-and-take marriage is one in which both partners honestly attempt

"I think we're doing a tremendous job of improving our marriage, dear."

to work through their problems in a mature, productive manner. They don't cling to illusions of a perfect marriage without problems because they humbly recognize that in spite of their best efforts, they are imperfect partners. Yet they work consistently to have a successful marriage because they know that they can be fulfilled and give fulfillment in spite of their imperfections. They know that the time spent in ironing out problems is worth every minute it may take. They have a positive attitude and a long-range outlook.

Attitudes Are Crucial

To change your marriage pattern from push and pull to give and take, examine the *inner* thoughts and attitudes that guide your *outer* behaviors. Like a computer, you tend to behave according to the attitudes you feed into your control center (your mind). If you feed a correct thinking pattern into your mind, you will be well on your way to achieving a successful marriage. Let's look first at essential attitudes for a give-and-take marriage and then examine resultant behaviors.

Case Study: Concern for Changing Only the Other Partner

As Phil and Carol stepped into my office, it soon was obvious that Phil didn't want to be there. He seemed quiet and resigned, however, as he helped Carol to a chair. Carol's eyes darted here and there, finally riveting on me, and we began. After some introductions and some chatter about the weather, we settled on the reason for their visit. "We need help," Carol told me. I assured them I fully intended to help them in every way possible and that we would be discussing ways each of them could begin to change themselves. At that point Carol focused her full attention on Phil and protested, "Yes, but Phil. . . ." I knew we were in for some long sessions. It was clear that Carol was the only one interested in improvement, and she was set to improve Phil, not herself.

A genuine desire to make things work.   When couples come to my counseling office, the first thing I look for is the desire to improve. This is crucial when you are in the "mending" business. When this factor is present in both the husband and wife, there is a high probability for success. Then both partners are willing and motivated to set realistic goals and to do whatever is necessary to achieve those goals.

Case Study: One Motivated Partner

Dave and Valerie came to me because Valerie insisted. Valerie had been pulling Dave for twenty years, and Dave had chronically pushed her away. Valerie was ready to change, and after each session would go home and put her new insights into practice. Dave made half-hearted stabs at changing his behavior, but only to appease Valerie. His motivation was low and he was quickly outdistanced by a wife who was willing to make a real effort to change herself.

Desire is closely linked to outcome. How badly do you want to reach your goal? Strong desire produces strong effort. In a give-and-take marriage, this means that both mates must be deeply committed to make things work. With such an attitude, the chances for success are high.

Flexibility toward one another.   Flexibility is central to a give-and-take marriage. Rigid dogmatism may cause a partner to become outspoken or withdrawn. Few people like to feel controlled, to be told constantly what to do.

Many couples mistakenly confuse flexibility with compromise, assuming that a flexible person has no convictions. They fail to see that people can have convictions and be flexible at the same time. One does not cancel out the other.

Case Study: Two Flexible People

Amy and Gary had a marriage that challenged their flexibility. Over the years, Amy had become a dedicated Christian, while Gary showed only minimal interest. Amy was outgoing, people-oriented, and very attached to her family. Gary did not share these attitudes. Yet both Amy and Gary claimed they had a satisfactory marriage. Gary explained why: "We knew in the beginning that if we developed a rigid mindset toward marriage we would end up either disillusioned or divorced." They explained that they made a joint decision to express their feelings while recognizing each other's need to have the final "say-so" about their own behavior. In other words, they decided to be flexible. Because of this, Amy and Gary developed a working rapport and a healthy respect for each other, despite the obvious differences in their personalities.

Sensitivity toward each other's feelings and needs. In a give-and-take marital pattern, each partner is aware of and actively cares about the needs of the mate. In this kind of arrangement, self-satisfaction takes a back seat. To ignore the needs of a partner is to feed the fires of discontent. Partners must demonstrate empathy for the needs of the spouse.

Empathy is a comprehension of the feelings and needs of another individual from that person's point of view. It is an active attempt to experience such needs and feelings. When spouses empathize, they try to understand one another from within, absorbing the inner nature of the mate. Empathy leaves little room for judgmental attitudes or self-centeredness. Rather, empathy is a giving process that involves a wholehearted effort to see things from the other person's point of view.

Many couples are afraid to show sensitivity toward each other for fear they will be "taken for a ride." Already feeling vulnerable, they also fear that being sensitive could backfire. But more often than not, empathy from one breeds empathy in the other. A caring attitude is contagious.

***An openness to feed-
back.*** Nobody's perfect. Who
would disagree with this? But
truth gets too close to home
sometimes, and a mate may refuse to listen when his/her
flaws are pointed out. Yet when
that mate points out flaws in
a spouse, the tone is harshly
critical and abrasive rather
than honest and caring.

Feedback from a caring, sensitive partner is priceless, and not
to be discarded. Taken as it is given, it can be "good medicine"
for an ailing relationship. Giving feedback without sensitivity is
likely to be a bust!

A give-and-take marriage makes room for constructive, honest
feedback. Growing partners know they haven't "arrived," and welcome opportunity to improve themselves and their marriage. They
welcome constructive input, knowing that others have valid per-
ceptions and reactions to their way of life. Growing partners aren't
threatened when attention is drawn to personal traits that offend
or annoy. They are willing to evaluate and apply the opinions of
others. This means that spouses are willing to say the words,
"You're right."

Attitudes Influence Behavior

Communicating with tact. Tact can make all the difference
when opinions are being aired. In marriage, this is particularly
true. Truth is more palatable to both parties when it is spoken in
a tactful manner, taking the other person's feelings into consideration. A rude, tactless remark can detour an otherwise beneficial
exchange down a deadend road. In a give-and-take marriage, tact-
lessness is out; diplomacy is in.

Does this mean couples should dance around sensitive issues
without getting to the real heart of the matter? Of course not. But
it does mean that for every rude way to make a point, there is a

more positive way to communicate. Individual needs can be stated in a constructive manner that will benefit both partners. This way, each person benefits twice.

One man greatly improved communication with his wife by changing statements like "Why don't you ever keep this den clean?" to "Let's pick up the clutter in the den." Or, he would say, "Do you want me to show you how this lock works?" rather than "Won't you ever learn how this lock works?" He shifted focus from her inefficiency to a solution.

Others have learned to avoid certain words and phrases at all costs. Sometimes, in irresponsible anger, spouses may shout: "I hate you," or "We'll just get a divorce." Words like these ring in the ears of the receiver long after arguments are settled. Tact requires strong self-discipline. The tongue is held in check. Only constructive words are spoken.

Using patience over and over.   Impatience is near the top of the list of reasons for marital stress. The case study below demonstrates how an exercise of patience on a husband's part effected a new beginning in his marriage:

Case Study: A Patient Husband

For two years, Karen and Jim argued constantly. They even came close to divorce. But Jim started looking at himself in terms of how much patience he had shown Karen and discovered he had really fallen short in that respect. It became clear to Jim that his impatience was a major factor in the prolonged arguments. Jim realized that neither Karen nor he would ever be perfect, and that if things were going to improve, someone must change. Jim had nothing to lose by showing patience. When Jim calmed down, Karen noticed the change and made efforts to slow down her own anger. They found that each time they made a conscious effort of their wills to be patient, they listened to each other better. This led to real hope, and they could see that bit by bit their relationship was improving.

Most couples admit to a lack of patience with each other, but fail to realize that patience can be acquired by using our God-given ability to *exercise our will.* He has given us the responsibility to make personal improvements through will power.

Jim and Karen knew they still had a way to go before they were consistently content. But with a patient heart, each of them determined to remain free from their old push-pull techniques.

Exercising kindness in mundane things.   One husband was overwhelmed (and overjoyed) at the response of his wife when he merely cleaned the table off one night after the meal. "She treated me like a king the rest of the night!"

A wife watched for a convenient time to bring her husband a tall glass of water while he was doing yard work. He was in a good mood all day because of it! She had made *him* feel significant by her small act of kindness.

It's not enough to wait until the "big" situations come up. They may be few and far between. It's the little things that count. There is no such thing as an insignificant act. Every act has significance. And it's very easy to find small ways to exercise kindness if you are looking. In a give-and-take marriage, partners are on the lookout every day for small favors they can do for each other.

Accepting imperfection but striving for perfection.   The "perfect marriage" is nothing more than a fantasy. Most of us could unhinge our imaginations long enough to dream up a "perfect marriage situation" for ourselves, but when we awake, the bubble will burst. This is not to say that we have to settle for mediocrity. We still can work toward perfection, realizing that we may have to travel through a few valleys and plateaus before we begin to climb mountains. In spite of our limitations, it is good to have lofty goals.

For example, a baseball player wants to get a hit each time he goes to bat. With every pitch he tries his best to get on base, knowing full well he will not get on base every single time. He knows that "outs" are a part of the game. Some of the best players expect to make an out seven out of every ten times they hit the ball! The odds are against them, but they don't quit! That would be irrational and immature. A good player knows he is going to be disappointed sometimes. He makes allowances for "outs."

Applied to marriage, the above illustration demonstrates that every day, every week, partners in a give-and-take marriage make efforts to have a perfect marriage. But when imperfections arise, they aren't caught by surprise. They know they may strike out sometimes, but they keep coming "back to home plate" anyway. They don't stop trying. Sometimes they have a winning streak, sometimes, they fall into a slump. When they take these ups and downs in stride, recognizing that this is a predictable part of life, they won't have the tendency to dwell on their problems, and make matters worse than they are.

Looking over these major characteristics of a give-and-take marriage, you will notice a distinct difference from the push-and-pull marriage. The game playing and manipulation of push-pull is replaced by common sense and cooperation. Figure 4 illustrates the differences between these two marriage patterns.

Figure 4 **Marriage Patterns**

Push and Pull	**Give and Take**
1. Arguments are destructive.	1. Arguments have a constructive purpose.
2. Communication is bogged down.	2. There is open communication.
3. Game playing is rampant.	3. Cooperation is real.
4. Control tactics are used.	4. Freedom is allowed.
5. Expectations are idealistic.	5. Expectations are realistic.
6. Problems are continually repeated.	6. Partners learn from their mistakes.
7. Selfish needs are considered first.	7. Other's needs are considered first.
8. There is a quitter's attitude.	8. Partners keep on trying.

7

Give-and-Take Anger

As you work toward a give-and-take marriage, one emotion above all others needs to be understood rightly — and that is anger. Anger, one of the most misunderstood emotions, also tends to be one of the most misused emotions. Generally, the misuse of anger is at the core of a push-pull marriage.

What Is Anger?

What is anger anyway? We talk about it, we feel it, and we are on the receiving end of it. But most people don't really know what it is! *Anger is nothing more than making an emotional stand for one's convictions.* * Becoming angry is an emotional reaction based on the need to hold firmly to a deeply-seated conviction. The conviction may be about a major issue or a trivial matter. For example, you may become angry when someone insults your personal dignity. By your anger, you are proclaiming the conviction that you are a person of worth who doesn't deserve to be insulted. Or you may become angry when your spouse does not respond immediately to a question you ask. In this case, you are holding the conviction that you should be spoken to immediately after you speak. Every time you feel angry, it is because one of your convictions has been violated. Anger is the emotion that accompanies your convictions.

When you view anger as taking a stand for your convictions, it doesn't sound negative. Rather, it seems more like a normal response. After all, it would be abnormal for a person to have no

*For further information see my book *Good 'n Angry* published by Baker Book House, 1983.

convictions. The only people who "never" get angry are the ones who have few or no firmly-held beliefs.

But here is the catch. Al-though it is normal for all peo-ple to have convictions, nearly all of us have had times when we have communicated our convictions in a destructive manner. We have already seen that when anger is not treated delicately it can lead to many problems. Ask anyone who has experienced either marital stress or divorce, and you will

TO PRESERVE MARRIAGE, TURN OFF WHEN NOT IN USE.

likely be told that anger was a much-abused emotion. Anger be-comes destructive when it is expressed in a way that clouds the issues and makes the individuals involved feel hurt or insulted.

We have all witnessed times when anger was sorely abused. Some couples remember times in their own marriage when one of them flew into a wild rage—yelling, screaming, and throwing ob-jects across the room. People familiar with these types of anger are not likely to think of it in positive terms.

Then there is another kind of anger experience. One spouse may decide not to talk to the other for hours. Angry silence may prevail for days. People who have had this experience also have a difficult time believing anything constructive can result from anger.

Most people have a hard time viewing anger in anything but negative terms. But in a give-and-take marriage, anger can actually be used to a couple's advantage. It's true. Anger can be a construc-tive tool when it is used properly.

Let's look at some ways anger is abused and see how each can bring nasty results:

Aggressive Anger

Loud and boisterous. It is the loud expression that gives an-ger a particularly bad name. Some people feel so overcome with frustration that yelling seems to be the only way to make a point.

Others add to yelling by flailing their arms dramatically or stomping their feet. The loud type of anger can even take on violent proportions and individuals may want to hit one another or kick holes in the walls. Name calling may be prevalent. When people get into the loud type of anger, they may begin to heap insult upon insult. There is a tendency to go on and on since impulse control decreases. These people will get red in the face and their blood pressure will climb. It is next to impossible to reason with an angry person aroused to this pitch.

Open and cutting.   Some people rarely "yell" or get physical when they are angry. Yet they still find avenues to vent anger and make others feel disgruntled. For example, a person with a strongly critical nature tends to express personal convictions in ways that make others feel put down. Likewise, sarcasm is a vehicle commonly used to deliver cutting remarks. Or, blame can be used to build oneself up, thereby using it as an effective tool to force the other person to change. Critical people may use gossip and they may be chronic complainers. They may be stubbornly inflexible and opinionated. In other words, anger can be expressed in many cutting ways that are not necessarily boisterous but tend to be equally as poisoning. Although this style of anger is not as raging as the chronic yellers, its users tend to lack commitment to the full communication process. Anger is used to "get things off my chest," but there is no attempt to hear other sides to the issues.

Passive-aggressive.   This kind of anger is exhibited by giving someone the silent treatment. Though no words are actually spoken, harsh feelings can be communicated with this behavior. The silent treatment can be abusive because it leaves the other person feeling totally disarmed and irritated. This, of course, is like extending an open invitation for prolonged aggravation. Silent anger can be as

"Ha!...You can stop trying to trick me into speaking to you because I'm very angry and I'm not going to do it."

destructive to a relationship as loud anger. The anger is there, but the angry person makes powerful attempts to keep the anger from being explored openly.

People who use passive-aggressive anger are afraid to expose their feelings because it makes them vulnerable and might lead to more personal adjustments than they counted on. In their attempts to avoid open conflict they actually can cause ill feelings to fester and grow.

Other forms of passive anger can include procrastinating, "forgetting," making halfhearted efforts, and being too preoccupied to notice the needs of another.

Each kind of abusive anger previously mentioned could be considered aggressive in one form or another. *Aggressive anger is defined as the emotion exhibited by persons who make a firm stand for their convictions without demonstrating a concern for needs of others.* Aggressive anger is the kind most often expressed in the push-pull marriage.

Assertive Anger

On the other hand, the give-and-take marriage is characterized by assertive anger. *Assertive anger is defined as the emotion exhibited by persons who take a firm stand for their convictions while at the same time being considerate of the needs of all involved.* In its purest sense, assertiveness means to put forward one's beliefs and values in a confident, self-assured manner. It involves a strong sense of commitment to what one knows to be right. Assertive anger is the only type of anger that works in a give-and-take relationship.

Figure 5 lists some of the differences between aggressive and assertive anger.

When people become aware of the vast differences between assertive anger and aggressive anger, most conclude they want to be more positive in their use of anger. But they may feel confused about how to be properly assertive. The most perplexing factor about assertive anger is the absence of "sounding" angry. When people are being properly assertive, they don't necessarily sound mad. So people will ask: "How can you call something anger when

Figure 5 **Types of Anger**

Aggressive	**Assertive**
Seeks to punish a person who does wrong	Seeks to help a person who does wrong
Does not care about the other person's point of view	Tries to be discreet and understanding
Is hard-nosed, immovable, and demanding	Is firm, yet willing to seek alternatives
Is condemning and judgmental	Recognizes that all have faults
Has high expectations of everyone	Knows that even the finest people are fallible
Cares more about what happens to self	Is concerned with self and others
Holds grudges	Knows the value of forgiving
Hates to admit one's own areas of weakness	Recognizes that everyone can be in a state of self-improvement

it doesn't seem like anger?" Here we go back to our original definition of anger. Though we have a common conception of anger as a vengeful and hostile spirit, that does not necessarily have to be the case. You can express anger by simply letting your beliefs be known in a firm way. This is why the Bible says to "be angry, and yet do not sin" (Eph. 4:26). That is, expressing anger is the responsible thing to do when you stand for your needs and for your convictions as long as you are not being sinful (destructive).

Assertive communication. When couples get into the habit of asserting themselves responsibly, there is less and less tendency to erupt with aggressive anger. It is possible to choose to be assertive rather than aggressive. Here are six ways you as a spouse can be assertive in your communication:

1. You can let your opinions be known. One of the most responsible things you can do in marriage is to let your thoughts be known to your mate. Neither party needs to stuff ideas and opinions in a suitcase. Couples have a much higher chance for success when they know what lies inside their partner's mind. (By the way, stating your opinions is much different than insisting on your own way.)

2. You can do what you know is right. One way to express yourself assertively is to do what you know is the correct thing to do. This is in keeping with the definition of anger as the tendency to take a stand for convictions. You may find yourself going against the opinion of the majority. But if you know that your actions are responsible, you are justified in expressing your feelings. An example of this would be when a wife leads her children in daily devotions even though her husband refuses to get involved in their spiritual development.

3. You can ask questions when you are confused. You may have noticed that people who do not ask clarifying questions when a confusing situation arises often display inappropriate anger at some later point. The give-and-take pattern includes asking questions when you feel "out in the dark" on any subject. That will take care of your current needs as well as prevent future aggressive episodes.

4. You can speak briefly and to the point. Have you noticed that aggressive anger tends to go on and on? Whether it is the ranting and raving anger or the silent treatment, aggressive anger is usually overdone. Using assertiveness, partners can be specific in what they want to say. With this type of communication, anger is out in the open but it doesn't linger to the point that it causes prolonged hurts.

5. You can request favors when needed. Many partners prefer not to ask the spouse to do a favor because they feel like they "shouldn't have to ask in the first place." But notice what happens when you don't ask favors that are legitimate and reasonable. You usually begin to carry grudges or hold resentments. This leads to inappropriate anger. Rather than letting your feelings fester and grow, go ahead and ask your favors. Even though you would prefer your spouse to be more spontaneous, it is better for you to make your requests known before you store up large amounts of anger.

6. You can set stipulations when necessary. There are times when spouses have the feeling that they are being taken advantage of. When this happens, the assertive, responsible thing to do is to declare your limits. "I'll be glad to help you with your work as soon as I finish what I'm doing." That action takes care of your needs, yet you are considerate of the needs of others.

In each of these six forms of assertiveness, two objectives are accomplished. First, you are holding firm to your own needs and convictions, and in so doing, you are likely to feel satisfied, knowing that you can help create a satisfying environment for yourself. Second, you are being considerate of the needs of others, which can serve to create a cooperative mood in the person with whom you are communicating. Both of you win.

Knowing When to Drop Anger

Expressing anger properly is important, but there are times when the most responsible thing to do is simply to drop anger altogether. In a give-and-take marriage, partners sense the limits to the amount of anger that can be expressed. They know when enough is enough.

Even well-adjusted couples know that in spite of their best efforts there will be times when the simplest statement of anger will ignite fireworks. The anger itself may not be wrong. Yet the timing can be completely off. When this is the case, one possible alternative is to drop the anger.

Dropping the anger is a delicate skill. Few people have mastered it. There is a fine line between dropping anger because of bad timing and repressing anger in such a way that bitterness foments to erupt later. Many people who say they are dropping anger are actually repressing it and letting it grow beneath the surface. They may not understand that when anger is dropped, it is gone for good; not simply set aside for another day.

There is an underlying assumption at work here: if you can drop anger (release it because it serves no useful function), it is possible to actually make choices about your emotions. Anger is a choice. You can choose to express it in an aggressive way. You can choose to be responsible with it by being assertive. Or you can choose to let it go. The latter choice is the one made least often in the push-pull marriage. But in the give-and-take marriage, this choice is made frequently.

Case Study: Controlled Anger

Joyce and her husband were very different from each other. Their temperaments didn't match, and their personal interests were miles apart.

Her husband had habits she didn't like at all. She had tried the explosive routine with no success. Things only got worse. At other times she was more subtly aggressive, becoming sarcastic and short with her husband. But she could see she was creating more problems than she was solving. So she tried to tone her anger down to a more moderate level. This was more satisfying and she found she could be more diplomatic in her statements. But even then, Joyce realized that she had to be careful not to overuse her anger. She knew if she spoke out too often, she might lose any effectiveness in her communication. So Joyce finally came to the conclusion that there would be times when the best choice was to choose to not indulge her anger. She knew that aggressive anger hardly ever brought good results. She even knew that there were times when assertive anger was ill-advised. As Joyce began to see anger as a choice, she felt a much stronger sense of self-control. And ultimately, Joyce contributed greatly to an improved situation by turning potentially bad episodes into constructive experiences.

Choosing your emotional expressions is not easy. Even logical people often allow their emotions to rule. Admittedly, it is difficult to shift gears when there is a pattern of emotions first, logic second. Yet it can be done! This is not to say that human beings should become machinelike in their personal interactions. It simply means that most of us could put more thought into the way we handle our emotions.

Anger can be as destructive or as constructive as a couple allows it to be. The give-and-take pattern allows for controlled (as opposed to indiscriminate) anger. Such partners realize that anger is too unpredictable to simply let it run loose with no restrictions. Rather than making anger an enemy to the marriage relationship, they work earnestly to use it as an ally.

8

Communication: More than Words

A major characteristic of a give-and-take marriage is mutual awareness of various communication patterns. As husband and wife face each day and each other, they keep their eyes and ears wide open. They don't want to miss a thing that could cause them to stumble. They know that they communicate to one another in almost everything they do. They accept the challenge to be as highly tuned in to each other as possible. This assures effective, orderly communication.

Communication Cues

Many couples complain: "We just don't communicate." Actually, this is not true. In any marriage all sorts of cues are part of the communication process. There is not one married couple that does not communicate *something* to one another. The challenge is to rightly understand the communication signals. For instance, you and your mate may be in the same room for an hour without talking. Is communication taking place? Yes, by all means. With some couples, this quiet time could indicate anger; they have tuned each other out. With other couples, it could mean that either they lead a dull life and there is nothing at the moment to talk about or they feel nothing in common. Or, perhaps, it could mean that the couple has an excellent rapport and words are not necessary to convey a warm feeling.

As much as 70 percent of human communication is conveyed in nonverbal messages. Words are not the final criteria of whether or not communication is taking place. To illustrate this, try to recall your favorite high school teacher. Can you remember two sentences this teacher actually spoke? Probably not. What you do remember, though, is the  general manner of a person's communication. Unspoken cues — a smile or a handshake — can make lasting impressions.

Depending on your personality style and your general pattern of living, the cues you give can vary in their meaning. Growing couples need to become responsive to the various communications taking place. Sensitivity to the following components of communication can help you to become a better communicator.

Tone of voice.   Tone of voice problems surface in several ways. Many people say they don't intend to nag, but they may sound nagging. Others intend to be firm, but they speak in weak timid tones. Still others may not be aware that their tone of voice makes them sound critical and condemning.

Case Study: Overpowering Tone

A few years ago, a short, handsome man came into my office seeking help with family problems. His chief complaint was that his wife and kids did not see him as being the loving, gentle man that he thought he was. He told of repeated attempts to tell his family members that he loved them, but somehow they just didn't respond. As he spoke, I realized that his tone of voice was a real problem. His rough bass voice didn't seem to fit his small stature at all. Although his words were not harsh, they sounded harsh. This man needed to work toward matching his voice to the emotion he wished to convey. When he wanted to be gentle, he needed to speak gently.

The sound of your voice sets the tone for ideas you wish to communicate. Before you can be taken seriously, your words and tones must match. Loving words are taken seriously when a loving, soft voice is used. Firm words are accepted when spokenly firmly. Your tone of voice probably will reflect your true feelings more than your actual words.

Emotional pitch. Emotional pitch makes a tremendous impact on the way words are received. At times, emotion is fully appropriate, but there are times when it can get totally out of hand. Many couples have learned through hard experiences that verbal messages are miscommunicated when the emotional level is wrong. Often the spouses make very necessary confrontations only to find themselves in the heat of an argument because emotions get out hand. Other times, anxiety can run so high that a normal topic of conversation is lost to emotional drainage.

Case Study: Pathetic Pitch

Frances discovered that her emotional nature almost cost her a marriage. Whenever she made a request of her husband, her entire demeanor took on a pitiful, sad whine. Though she didn't mean to, she repulsed her husband to the point that he wanted to avoid further contact with her. If he ever confronted Frances, even mildly, she would break down in tears. Her emotional nature communicated a fragile temperament, which was based on her low self-esteem. It also communicated a total absorption with herself. When she learned to speak with emotional pitch agreeable to her words, she found her husband much more receptive.

Personal bearing and expression should be parallel or consistent with the words you speak. That cornerstone must be laid if your communications are to be productive. When expression and words do not agree, confusion will likely result.

Nonverbal Communication

Silence. Contrary to what some couples may believe, silence communicates much. Often when one marriage partner is silent, the other interprets the silence as rejection or lack of concern. One woman described her husband as self-centered and uncaring because he came home from work each night and sat in his easy chair, saying nothing. But later it became apparent that this man had so little experience communicating openly that his silence was actually caused by a feeling of ineptitude. Because he did not communicate his feelings openly, his wife was left to try to guess his inner thoughts.

Silence can be very threatening. When an individual remains silent too often or becomes silent in crucial discussions, the spouse can feel shunned or insulted. Some partners use silence to communicate disfavor, anger, or disinterest. This tactic seriously harms good communication. Other partners, however, are silent by nature. They may have a very subdued temperament. In such cases, they need to recognize the spouse's desire to hear from them regularly.

Listening.   With some people, listening is a lost factor in their communication style. They think of communication as being something that is emitted. Yet listening is probably the most important component in the communication process. Think of this: God created us with two ears and one mouth. What we hear is twice as important as what we have to say.

Some people have a need to talk and talk and talk some more. Usually, talkative persons communicate more than they realize. Frequently, an extra-talkative person lacks sensitivity or concern for another person's well-being. The talker is obsessed with self. But a gabby person could also communicate nervousness. Talkativeness could indicate a deep-rooted sense of insecurity, or sometimes, it simply means that the individual is happily excited.

Case Study: The Overwhelmer

In one group therapy session, a particularly talkative lady we'll call Gwen told the group why she was distressed. "People don't seem to like me as much as I like them." When asked for their response, the group members helped Gwen realize she was a very overwhelming person. She so dominated conversation that people wanted to avoid her. When Gwen heard this, she was stunned. She certainly had no intention of being overwhelming.

The next week when the group reconvened, I was concerned because Gwen was not in her seat as usual. I stepped out into the waiting room and found Gwen absorbed in conversation with another person. Instead of Gwen doing all the talking, she had been the steady listener for at least fifteen minutes! That had to be a record for her! When I asked her about it later, she remarked that she had considered seriously the feedback given her the week before. She told me she had always wanted to be a sensitive person. And since she had learned that her talkative nature projected the wrong image, she was making an honest effort to be more the person she wanted to be. Awareness of her problem made the difference for her.

Touching. The amount of touching between spouses tells a lot about their feelings toward one another. The couple that touches freely usually has a comfortable style of expressing love. The couple that finds it hard to touch will likely have difficulty communicating openly. The touch of a hand provides a sense of security to a relationship. It gives spoken words added meaning. I often encourage couples who are having communication difficulties to take notice of how much touching exists between them. After they begin to take notice, they usually will conclude one of two things: Either they don't touch each other enough or there is too much touching. In one case, distance between the two exists. In the other, there is a problem with smothering.

A healthy amount of touching might include a friendly pat on the back when a compliment is given. It may include an occasional hug or kiss for no apparent reason. Or a couple could sit next to each other occasionally during evenings at home instead of splitting off to different ends of the house. Many couples enjoy snuggling in bed even when sexual relations do not occur.

A meaningful touch can set an atmosphere that makes open communication come naturally.

Eye contact.   Have you ever talked with someone who won't look you straight in the eye? It's unnerving, isn't it! When this happens, what is communicated to you? If you are like most people, you would interpret poor eye contact as disinterest. Or it may mean that the other person is preoccupied. Poor eye contact does not convey a caring nature or a desire for open communication.

If you want successful verbal exchanges in your marriage, eye contact is a must. Good eye contact indicates concern and a genuine desire to understand your mate's point of view. Eye contact brings security to your interactions. Without it, your spouse may feel uncertain that real communication is actually taking place.

Style of dress.   The mode of dress invariably communicates a message. Blue jeans say one thing, and a suit or a dress another. A couple who wears their "Sunday best" out to dinner communicates that this occasion is special. On Saturdays, they may communicate a feeling of ease by wearing the casual clothes they usually wear on weekends.

Potentially, troubles can erupt when couples are not sensitive to what they communicate in their dress. A woman who wears provocative clothing in public may be communicating that her husband is not the only man she is interested in. A husband who appears chronically unkempt may communicate disregard for his wife's preferences. Or, some people can dress so stiffly that they communicate an aloofness or a "better-than-thou" attitude. However a couple chooses to dress, it is best to consider desires of both the husband and the wife. It is part of the give-and-take communication process.

Communication Tips

Along with an increased awareness of these nonverbal clues, you can practice specific procedures to make your communication patterns flow more smoothly. These six practical tips will allow you to move another step away from the push-pull marriage and closer to the give-and-take marriage.

1. Make open communication a high priority. Practice the art of speaking openly and frequently with one another. This will un-

clutter your communication, and let your mate know what your thoughts and feelings are so there will be little question. The more you work to provide clarification the less confusion you and your mate will have.

2. Be attentive to your spouse's communication. Most people assume that they are being attentive when they listen to the words spoken by another person. Granted, listening is a very important part of attentiveness but it doesn't stop there. Attentiveness "registers" nonverbal messages also. The whole person is noticed. The communicating couple wants to understand the feelings behind facial and body expressions. Only when you pick up all the cues given by your spouse will you be a complete listener.

3. Be attentive to your own communication style. You need to become as consistent as possible in the way you communicate. Are you aware of your own nonverbal communication practices? If people perceive you as unfriendly it may be your tone of voice. Listen to yourself. If you are not taken seriously, perhaps it may be because you present yourself in a self-deprecating manner. Your goal is to be consistent in the verbal as well as nonverbal cues you give to others.

4. Accept feedback from your spouse. No one will ever be a perfect mate. But we all can improve. No doubt your spouse could spot some of your special areas that need improvement. Be open to suggestion. Don't be insulted at feedback about inconsistency in your communication style. After all, as husband and wife you are teammates (not opponents) trying to make things work better for the team. (A word of encouragement: When you give feedback to your spouse, be certain it is done in a constructive manner. There is no room for offensive feedback in a growing marriage.)

5. Set aside time each week to clear up any potential problem areas. Marital conflicts easily erupt when couples don't take the time out to discuss the issues sanely. One couple successfully handled their potential arguments by setting aside every Thursday night as "beef night." If either of them had a "beef" it was saved until Thursday. When the time came, they discussed any issues that had bothered them during the week. By setting aside a specific time to iron out their gripes, this couple discovered two things: First, they tended to be more rational in their communication style.

Consequently, they kept petty issues from getting out of hand. Second, they found that they tended to dismiss a large number of "beefs" during the week because they no longer were important. Also, by having a time set aside to air out any problems, this couple found that they were much more aware of their communication patterns.

By making open communication a top priority, you will find that tug-of-war sessions occur less frequently and that you have moved another notch closer to enjoying a meaningful marriage.

As you achieve success in monitoring your nonverbal communication style, you will be ready to tackle the further suggestions for communication given in the next chapter.

9

Give-and-Take Communication

Some people may assume that those who come to me for counseling are flaky, off-the-wall types. But that is not true. Individual or couples who come for counseling often are healthier than most people because they are willing to look at areas of their lives that need improvement.

Case Study: Communication Problem

Chuck and Marilyn were average, middle-class people. Chuck worked as a lab technician and Marilyn sold cosmetics part time in addition to caring for the children. Their marriage wasn't in serious trouble, but they did want to improve the way they handled conflicts. It seemed they mishandled angry situations, and they knew their marriage was too good to let this problem get the best of them.

We spent a couple of sessions talking about their goals for marriage and how goals affected their attitudes. We discussed their individual self-images and how this influenced marriage. We then approached the subject of communication. To this point, they were receptive and willing to discuss the issues fully. But when I suggested that they needed to examine their communication style more closely, both Chuck and Marilyn balked. Almost in unison they explained they had no problem talking with each other. (It was apparent that they were *very* open with each other.) They said that if anything in their marriage wasn't a problem, it was communication.

I helped them understand, however, that the ability to speak openly with each other does not necessarily mean perfect communication exists. I told them speaking openly was a good start, but communication involves much more than words. The techniques Marilyn and Chuck used reflected inner attitudes that needed examination. As we explored av-

enues of better communication skills, a whole new world of sharing
opened up for them. They found that once they gained proficiency in
outward communication, inner problems like anger diminished. They
learned that an active speech pattern doesn't necessarily make good
communication happen, and that what you do while you are speaking
determines the success or failure of your interchanges.

Your outward style of communicating reflects inner attitudes
toward your marriage. As you are working to improve your inner
attitudes, you will enhance your efforts by concentrating also on
your outward skills. When your outward skills improve, your inner
attitudes will likewise improve. And as your attitudes brighten, it
will be easier to put the skills into use. The process feeds itself,
and interpersonal growth accelerates.

The story of "My Fair Lady" is a favorite of mine. The fussy
professor who takes in a cockney from the East end of London
and transforms her into a high-society lady illustrates the relationship of outward skills to inner attitudes. His approach was
twofold. First, he had to teach her how to talk and behave like a
lady. He spent long hours teaching her how to communicate like
a proper person. Second (and most difficult), he wanted her to not
only talk and behave like a lady, but also to think like a lady. He
knew this would come only after her external crudeness was con-
quered. Of course the story ended with the heroine becoming a
lady in both words and thought.

On your road toward improvement you will also encounter a
twofold task. Both your inner and outer lives must be involved to
bring the completion you want. The guidelines in this chapter will
give structure to your outward communication style. But you will
notice quickly that they also make a great difference in your in-
ward attitudes. Learn to build your speaking patterns on a solid
foundation, and you will achieve greater success in your efforts
to have a give-and-take marriage. As you read these guidelines,
look for opportunities for personal improvement.

1. Develop a sense of timing. Spouses frequently have important
things to talk about, but they can pick the worst possible moment
to bring up the subject. For example, if a wife needs to discuss a
problem about the kids with her husband, it is not wise to bring
it up when he is rushing out the door to go to an important meet-

ing. In good communication each mate considers the other's mood and frame of mind. Look to your spouse's mental and emotional climate to determine how and when you will approach discussions, just as you would dress according to the climate outside.

2. Share from an unselfish heart. Some people communicate openly only when they feel a personal need. Otherwise, they are not interested. This kind of communication comes from a position of selfishness. In a give-and-take marriage, selfishness is out and consideration is in. Your communication can be motivated by the desire to create an atmosphere of togetherness. You can recognize that your chances for good rapport increase when you are not defensive. You are willing to put your thoughts and feelings on the line. Your chief concern is harmony.

3. Be willing to give your mate more compliments than complaints. Sometimes open communication doesn't occur until a problem comes up. Then the discussion becomes little more than a gripe session. Naturally, this doesn't do much to encourage the harmony that is so necessary in a give-and-take marriage. Do you know the best way to be taken seriously when you have a complaint? You first have to establish your reputation as a positive, pleasant person. If you spend a large percentage of your time griping and criticizing, your complaints won't carry much weight. Your mate will just think: "Here we go again, what's wrong this time?" To be taken seriously by your mate, you need to make it known that you prefer to look on the positive side of life. Find ways to compliment your spouse. Look for pleasant subjects to discuss. Be someone who seeks the best in others. Because you will be a more attractive person, you will carry more clout if anything arises that calls for confrontation or reprimanding.

4. Listen; then consider feelings behind mate's words. Have you ever felt that discussions with your spouse are more like a debate than a real discussion? Spouses sometimes complain that when they discuss issues, one partner acts like a prosecuting attorney and the other like the defense. Both spend too much energy defining the issues and tossing out theories; neither sufficiently considers the feelings of the other. In your efforts to understand one another, seek first to comprehend your mate's feelings. Feelings can communicate much more than words. On a practical level,

this means when your spouse looks dejected, you can comment on the feeling you notice (i.e., "You look sad, tell me about it"). Or, if your spouse is mad, rather than being threatened by the anger, seek to be understanding (i.e., "Maybe we don't agree on this subject, but I know you are angry and I am willing to consider your feelings").

5. Ask clarifying questions when you are confused. It is amazing how often couples will get bogged down in frustrating discussions because they won't stop to clarify the issues. Many couples will go around and around about nothing, allowing tense feelings to build. Such discussions call for one spouse to take the initiative and get the communication on track (i.e., "Okay, let's slow down and figure out what we are talking about. Would you share with me what it is you want me to understand?"). By bringing discussions down to earth, you can keep your emotions from going into orbit.

6. Seek to be an "understander," not an answer-giver. A common tendency of people involved in discussion is a readiness to give answers (i.e., "Why don't you . . ." or "maybe you should think about . . ."). While not intending to, some people do come across as possessing superior knowledge. This creates a one-up one-down style of communicating. In any relationship, the goal is to communicate from a co-equal position. When you chronically give suggestions and answers in your discussion, you may imply that you don't think your mate is capable of figuring out the issues. But when your goal is to show understanding, you can imply a sense of respect for that person's feelings and a sense of trust in your spouse's capability to come to grips with the needed solutions.

7. Be willing to respond constructively to your partner's point of view even if you disagree. Have you ever noticed how some people are terrific conversationalists as long as you agree with them? Their idea of good communication is mutual pats on the back. But this doesn't have to be the case. Good communication can exist even when you and your mate come from different points of view. You may find that you can learn something new by considering a point of view different from your own. Rather than being threatened by differentness, you can capitalize on it.

8. Stay away from using imperative terms. Words like *should*,

ought to, have to, supposed to, must, and *had better* can shut down communication lines completely, if used too often. Those words imply a superior way of thinking and doing. They imply only one direction a subject may be approached. They can betray a close-minded nature. This is not to say that a person should never use imperative terms. After all, some things are black and white. Yet as a rule, it is more profitable to have flexibility in your communication.

9. Avoid exaggeration. In your efforts to keep communication on track it is wise to stay away from absolute words like *always* and *never.* These words invite debate over side issues. They cause discussions to lose their original distinction. Usually, nothing is as black and white as these words would suggest. Also, you will have better communication when you stay away from superlatives ("That's the dumbest statement I have ever heard"). By making extreme statements you invite your mate to veer off course and discuss something irrelevant to the original subject.

10. When discussing problems, keep their importance in perspective. It is amusing to hear what some couples argue about. I have known couples who argued endlessly about the husband leaving a dirty dish in the sink. I have known couples who will brood and fume for hours because the wife wasn't cheery enough when she said hello to her husband. Some spouses are masters at making mountains out of molehills. About 95 percent of all marital arguments could be resolved quickly if both would accept minor irritants which are a normal part of married life. In most minor disagreements, a brief statement of your opinion or your feeling is all that is needed. Before waging an all-out war with one another, consider first the seriousness of the problems.

11. When feelings get in the way, be willing to table the issue until the mood is better. Self-control is essential in discussion. No marital partners will totally agree on every issue. Emotions become a factor from time to time. If you are having a hard time with your emotions regarding a particular topic, tell your spouse you need a short break to collect yourself. But don't use this as a ruse to avoid the issue. Make sure you return with the full intention of closing the discussion.

12. Don't attack your mate. A major goal in communication is

to speak from a co-equal position. One of the best ways to throw your efforts off track, though, is to speak from an "attack" position. This encourages the push-pull pattern to build. When a spouse attacks with insults, name-calling, or extreme criticism, a battle for superiority is launched. Problems are created because the attacked partner is cornered in a defensive position and has the desire to fight back. A circular motion usually begins. In contrast to the attack approach, couples in a give-and-take-marriage know the vital place for direct talk without put-downs. They are motivated to express thoughts and opinions openly, and they also are willing to listen with a receptive ear.

13. Remember, winning is not the goal. When you are in a discussion with your mate, do you have a tendency to keep the upper hand? Some people hate to lose. Consequently, a personal encounter is viewed as a contest. Rather than recognizing that different people have different notions, such people are on a crusade to convince anyone who is not "properly enlightened" about the correct way to think. In their efforts to be convincing, these spouses are actually trying to win a battle ("convince" originally meant "to conquer"). But notice the problem this creates: Where there is a winner, there is also a loser. And in marriage, when you win a battle, you are forcing your own teammate to lose! Remember, as spouses, you are on the same team. Don't destroy the other half of your team.

14. Remember: your mate is only human — and so are you. Often couples have lofty goals for marriage. And they should, because high goals are positive motivators. But while you are pursuing your goals, keep in mind that both you and your mate will not be perfect. We all make mistakes, sometimes repeatedly. This means that you can count on your spouse to goof. And you will also goof. There will be times when the goofs are really bad. But don't let this catch you off guard. In the communication process, your spouse might not always be a good listener. Neither will you. Your spouse won't consistently say what you want to hear. Neither will you. Since we are all imperfect, however, this need not signal disaster. Look at your humanness as an opportunity for improvement!

You will notice that these fourteen points on communication

are common-sense guidelines. Most people have the ability to use common sense. But sometimes, it is set aside for personal gain. Concentrate on the task so you will be successful in your efforts to apply common-sense communication.

10

When Opinions Clash

Do you know what is one of the most difficult challenges married couples can face? It is "knowing" you are correct when your spouse "knows" you are incorrect. Talk about a tight spot! Faced with that dilemma, you can either insist on your point of view or humbly bow to your spouse's. You are both certain you are right, yet each of you has a completely different opinion.

When opinions clash, most couples argue. They get into the push-pull pattern. A wife, for example, may persistently try to pull her husband into agreements only to be pushed away. Then the roles switch. The wife becomes defensive as the argument shifts to the husband's point of view. He becomes the puller, insisting that his opinion is correct. Now, she pushes him away. A stalemate develops simply because they both refuse to yield.

Case Study: Two Stubborn "Rights"

John and Sharon had been married nineteen years. They frequently enjoyed moments when they felt close to each other. Overall, they felt that their marriage was good. But they had one recurring problem. Both of them were stubborn. Both hated to admit they were wrong, and furthermore, each resented that the *other* person wouldn't say "you're right."

John had definite but good ideas about family living, open communication, and consistent support in the marriage relationship. But he was very opinionated and vocal about how a wife should treat her husband. For example, he believed that when he and Sharon had disappointments they should sit down and talk things over. He expected Sharon to create a pleasant atmosphere when he was at home in the evening. In talking with him, it became clear that he had many convictions about what his wife ought to do to make the marriage work. And he was very proud that his opinions were logical and even biblically based.

But John had a problem. When Sharon failed to act according to his standards, he tended to respond like a correcting parent. He frequently would admonish her about the error of her ways. At first, he would mildly suggest a "right" way for her to behave. If she failed to meet the standard, his voice became firmer. Eventually, he became obnoxiously gruff. John's opinions were correct technically, but he stated them in a way that contributed to discord.

Meanwhile, Sharon had her own opinions (correct, of course!). When John argued his point, Sharon retorted that he needed to let her live life her own way. She would point out how wrong it is for a husband to impose himself on his wife. Sharon, too, had firm ideas about right and wrong. She had strong opinions regarding the role of the husband and was determined to hold tenaciously to her point of view. She "knew" she was correct.

Can you see the problem this presents? Each spouse had opinions that could be logically defended. Both felt they were "right" and both argued stubbornly about the other person's need to change. Each hoped the other would give in and apologize eventually.

The problem John and Sharon faced is common. Whenever two people have an open exchange of ideas and opinions, sooner or later they'll reach a point of disagreement when both parties believe they are correct. When this point is reached, there is a strong need for the pattern of give-and-take.

A Meaty Issue

To help us come to grips with this problem let's examine an incident that unfolded in the church at Corinth as recorded in I Corinthians, chapter 8. The Christians in Corinth were given to petty squabbling. They either enjoyed arguing or had a hard time knowing how to handle varying opinions. Paul comments in this first letter to the Corinthians that the church consisted of both carnal and spiritual Christians (read I Cor. 3:1 – 3). That is, some of the Christians were growing spiritually while many others too closely resembled non-Christians (carnal).

In the eighth chapter of his letter to the church, Paul discussed a particular problem. The Corinthian Christians debated whether it was permissible to eat meat previously offered as a sacrifice to idols. Some felt that this was harmless but others felt this action spiritually defiled the meat. Both factions were convinced they were right and the opposing view was wrong. Does this sound familiar?

One group of Christians felt that freedom of conscience would allow them to eat the meat that had been first offered to idols. The meat tasted good, and they knew God had created it. They realized idols were meaningless and felt it was irrelevant that pagans had offered the meat to idols before selling it on the market. The meat sold at discount prices, and this group had no qualms about buying and eating it.

The second faction within the church strongly opposed eating meat offered to idols. Paul refers to this group as having a weaker conscience than the rest. These Christians were afraid that eating this "defiled" meat would displease God and felt their fellow believers were condoning idol worship. Therefore, each group took a rugged stand for what they felt was right, but neither was ready to budge an inch.

Can't you picture their church conference on the issue? Their meetings could easily have turned into a series of heated outbursts with each side throwing verbal barbs at the other. Each group claimed superior knowledge. Neither side was willing to back down. So they appealed to Paul. "Let's find out what Paul thinks about this."

Paul went on record that it was acceptable for Christians to eat meat offered to idols (cf. I Cor. 8). He agreed that the people who feared God's condemnation were ill-informed. Yet in responding to their question, he forced the two factions to examine a more pressing problem.

Paul told both factions they were wrong in the way they handled the dispute. He correctly diagnosed their cardinal problem as a wrong view of priorities. Both groups thought knowledge was the key factor in settling their disagreement. Paul begins the chapter by saying, "We know that we all have knowledge. Knowledge makes arrogant." Hold onto that phrase "knowledge makes arrogant."

What did Paul mean? He was telling the disgruntled people in the church that he knew both groups felt they had the correct knowledge. But he pointed out that their knowledge had become their enemy. Each faction was so intent on cramming their "knowledgeable" opinions into the "errant" persons that both had become arrogant. Each assumed a position of false superiority over the opposing side. They were critical and condescending to each other. Paul emphasized that the main issue was not to decide who was right and who was wrong. He wanted to lift them to an even higher priority: the priority of love.

Read verse one again, and notice what else Paul says: "We know that we all have knowledge. Knowledge makes arrogant, but love edifies." The principle is clear. When there is an argument where both parties feel absolutely correct, we are not to sacrifice fellowship just to prove that we are right. And the primary question we are to ask is this: "What is the most loving thing that I can do when we disagree?" Love must get priority consideration over "proving" we are right.

Paul reiterates this theme: "If I speak with the tongues of men and of angels, but do not have love, I have become a noisy gong or a clanging symbol. And if I have the gift of prophecy and know all mysteries and all knowledge; and if I have all faith, so as to remove mountains, but do not have love, I am nothing" (I Cor. 13:1 – 2). In other words, it just doesn't matter much how right I am if I'm unloving. No amount of correctness gives me or anyone else an excuse to condemn or to speak haughtily.

Accepting the Challenge

You might say, "I agree that love must be a primary consideration. But I wish my spouse could understand this principle." But wait! It's not your job to impose your new knowledge onto your spouse. The challenge to put love first is issued directly to you.

Look back at I Corinthians 8, verses 7 through 9. Paul wanted to make sure that his readers were not concerned only about how others should think. He explains that not all people will share the same points of view all the time. And because you can't expect everyone to share your insights, no matter how correct they are, it is up to you — not the other person — to break the deadlock.

"I'm right!" "No, I'M RIGHT!"

The point is this. You are free to think and believe whatever you wish. In fact, you are encouraged to hold firm beliefs. But if your beliefs rile another person to the point of endangering the relationship between the two of you, it's time to reconsider your course. Arguments aren't worth the heartache they usually cause. Consequently, do what you can to keep love alive. Don't become a stumbling block. Don't be so stubborn that all communication breaks down.

I've met several couples who never seem to agree on anything. No matter how small the issue, they frequently disagree. You've probably known couples with this problem. This kind of standoff creates a touchy situation. But it doesn't mean all hope for a good relationship is lost. By placing love before all else, you can still have a rewarding relationship with your mate in spite of your differences.

See how the principle of loving first and foremost can help break the push-pull pattern? Loving sensitivity is a key ingredient that leads toward the pattern of give-and-take. By applying this principle you exhibit the kind of flexibility that is a cornerstone in the give-and-take marriage. Don't hold so firmly to your opinions that you drive yourself and your mate toward total frustration. Rather, lovingly seek to meet the needs of your mate. This is not to say you should "drop" all your opinions. That could lead to chaos and disaster. What it does mean is that sensitivity comes first.

Minimizing the Risks

At this point, you may be wincing. You think: "Okay, I know that love is the right way to go. But what happens if my spouse takes advantage of me?" Good question.

To be honest, there is a risk involved in setting your knowledge aside in favor of a decision to be loving. But any great feat involves risk. In this case, the risk is that your mate may continue to be stubborn. Your mate may not see the need to let go of knowledge in favor of love. If this happens, you will be in a vulnerable position. You may be the only one in your twosome who is trying.

Case Study: Unreciprocated Love

For twelve long years Larry had been involved in a push-pull marriage. He and his wife constantly disagreed. Larry was totally frustrated because he genuinely wanted to be a good husband. As he grew in his Christian faith, Larry became convinced that he had put too much emphasis on proving his opinions. He realized that his willingness to verbally "slug it out" with his wife was taking them downhill. Besides, he was rarely successful in changing his wife's opinion. For all his logic, he couldn't make her understand things from his point of view.

So, in an effort to stabilize his marriage, he consciously decided to apply the love principle found in I Corinthians 8. Rather than being insistent when he and his wife disagreed, he would state his opinion just once or twice, and then back away from the argument. He was adamant only on the most important issues. Larry told his wife he wanted peace at home, even if it meant he would have to refrain from expressing his strong opinions. Inwardly, Larry hoped his wife would catch on and follow his lead.

For the most part, Larry found arguments were fewer and shorter in duration. This encouraged him. Things were moving in the right direction. But, to his dismay, his wife seemed as opinionated as ever. In spite of his daily efforts to be a better mate, his wife still didn't share Larry's new flexibility. It seemed that while Larry was improving himself she was on "automatic pilot" at the same old altitude. At this point, Larry reviewed his options. He realized that he could return to his former stubborn behavior. After all, if she refused to change why should he be the one to make all the sacrifices? Yet, as he thought this over, he remembered how miserable he was during their standoffs. So Larry concluded that while he would pay a higher price for a good marriage than his wife would, it was worth the effort. All things considered, love (even unreciprocated love) was the way to go.

Fortunately, not everyone will have the same experience as Larry's. In a true give-and-take marriage, both partners are willing to compromise. Both are willing to risk becoming vulnerable. As one partner shows improvement, the other will be influenced to respond in a like manner. Of course, this won't be the case 100 percent of the time. But there will be a shared sense of responsibility.

To make love, not knowledge, your higher priority, consider the following points:

1. The *way* you communicate your thoughts is equally (if not more) important than *what* you wish to communicate.

2. Sometimes the smartest thing you can say to your spouse is "You're right," or "I think I can understand your point of view."

3. Always be aware of where you are going in a discussion. Are you moving toward increased harmony? If not, rethink your actions and words.

4. You can choose your mode of communication. That is, you can choose to be stubborn or you can choose to be understanding.

5. A year from now, even a week from now, it probably won't matter whether or not you were correct.

6. You don't have to repeat your opinions fifteen times during an argument. Your spouse often knows your opinions before you even speak them.

7. You are likely to have a more powerful influence at home when you establish the fact that love is your first priority.

8. Even if you don't succeed in influencing your spouse, you will still benefit from living in a loving manner. All things considered, this is better than being dogmatic and bitter.

Of course, to live according to this principle of love first and knowledge second, it is important that you know how to love, which we will discuss in the next chapter.

11

Give-and-Take Love

What is love? This question has intrigued philosophers since the beginning of time. It certainly is an important question, because your definition of love will directly influence your attitudes and mannerisms in any relationship, especially marriage.

Many individuals will say, "I don't love my spouse anymore." Something happens to cause these people to switch their feelings from positive to negative. They believe they have lost hope for a satisfactory marriage. But what they really need is a different perspective on love.

The need for love is engrained in all of us. We all want special attention from someone significant. This need is normal. In fact, the need for love is behind the push-pull pattern of marriage. If love is not given in a satisfactory way, we are prone to resort to a push or pull technique to force love from our spouse. Consequently, our challenge is to thoroughly understand this emotion so we can give it and take it in a way that helps marriage grow.

When both partners work simultaneously to have the right perspective on love, their efforts to have a give-and-take marriage flourish. Each partner experiences rewards that come from being on both the giving and the receiving end of love. Throughout their entire married lives, couples can work to find new and meaningful ways to put love into the heart of their relationship.

In today's world, however, the pursuit of love can pose problems. Because there are so many different meanings attached to the word, one person seeking love may have entirely different notions than another. Even in marriages, the words *"I love you"* can mean something completely different to each partner. Let's

examine four basic types of love. From these you can focus on areas of your love life that need work.

Erotic love.   It is popular to view love only as a sensual experience. In today's vernacular the word *erotic* has come to denote fleshly desire and lust. Erotic love, however, can also include romance and sentimentality. It is the type of love most often depicted by song writers and novelists. Erotic love is usually controlled by unpredictable physical needs.

Many people with a Christian background or strong moral training consider erotic love as evil. And they have reasons for this. They have seen the overwhelming emphasis our culture places on the purely physical aspects of sex. They see television and movie screens portraying erotic love as an ultimate experience. They note that even birthday cards tease about purely physical sex! They are correct in saying that eroticism has been blown out of proportion, and, in many cases, misrepresented and misunderstood.

But it would be in error to categorically dismiss erotic love as wrong love. There is a special place for it within the context of a Christian marriage. The Song of Solomon unfolds the thrilling aspects of this type of love. Within the boundaries of a Christian marriage, erotic love is not a sleazy infatuation with physical sex.

Rather, it can be a wonderful emotional high that brings excitement into the marriage. When understood as a gift from God to marriage partners, erotic love can be the physical expression of a tender, caring sentiment toward one another. Certainly, this is not the only love needed in a good marriage. But it is a normal and healthy desire in courtship and marriage.

Belongingness love. We all have a need to belong. From earliest childhood to latest adulthood, people like to know they have an established position. Consider the cozy feeling you have when after a trip you return home to your favorite easy chair or to the "only" bed that sleeps right. An inner glow comes from knowing you have an established position of security. This is where you belong.

Marriage is an obvious way to meet an individual's need for belonging. When you have a mate, you have an identity. You are no longer a loner. You are part of a team. There is a sense of emotional refuge when you experience "belongingness" love. It is the desire for a belongingness love that prompts most people to marry in the first place. When the need to belong is met, there is the calm assurance you have someone to lean on. You have someone to go to. But when this need is not met, you may feel empty. Void. You may feel utterly rejected.

Companionship love. This kind of love exists in any rewarding, interpersonal relationship. It is the type of love that expresses itself in a feeling of camaraderie, in a willingness to be friends and really communicate. In contrast to an infatuation which borders on human worship, companionship love is accompanied by feelings of relaxation and ease. You know you are in the soothing presence of someone comfortable and you feel free to be yourself.

You can readily grasp how important companionship love is to a growing marriage. It is at the very core of a give-and-take relationship. On one hand, there is an openness and willingness to share thoughts and feelings with your mate. On the other hand, there is a desire to listen with understanding to things that are important to your spouse. Companionship love takes two people who are cooperative and responsive in their relationship.

Agape love. This last type of love is the deepest and most difficult to achieve. It is different from the other three types of love in that it doesn't rely on feelings. Rather, agape love is an exercise of the will. It is a totally selfless act of living in direct accord with biblical principles. It is a clear demonstration you are giving your love life over to the direction of God. Rather than emotional in origin, agape love is divinely inspired. It is love that is given by sheer willpower, even when the feelings are not present.

Agape love is the ingredient that gives an otherwise average marriage distinction. Whereas erotic love, belongingness, and companionship are important factors in a marriage relationship, agape love brings completion. It keeps flowing even when the emotional highs stop. On a practical level, this means that when you are at the end of a bad day, you can choose to be loving in spite of your weariness. When you disagree with your spouse, love can still be a part of your relationship because you can choose to remain committed and pursue harmony. When you experience serious trials, agape love can keep your marriage going even when the other three types of love are missing.

Agape love is the love most often discussed in the Bible. It is contrary to human nature since our first tendency is to please self. Consequently, for agape love to become a dominant part of your marriage, you must be ready to use extra measures of your willpower. When agape love is firmly established, it can become the foundation on which the other three types of love are laid and enhanced.

Case Study: Agape Love

A Christian man named Roger once hit the very depths of despair in his marital life, yet ultimately he was able to keep his marriage alive because of his agape love. His story went like this: Roger had met Denise in the early stages of his career. You wouldn't exactly call their romance a whirlwind because they spent over a year getting acquainted. They socialized frequently, and found they enjoyed similar forms of entertainment. They liked each other's company. They frequently talked in depth about their most personal beliefs, including religion, politics, and family living. Their points of disagreement were only minor. Besides, they found it stimulating to talk about challenging questions. In addition, they spent time getting to know each other's family members and found ready rapport among them. In short, it seemed like Roger and Denise were well on their way to a satisfying marriage.

But once they married, things changed. Twelve years into their marriage, after having a son, Denise decided to return to work. She had experience with complex business machines, and readily found work with a computer firm as a "trouble shooter" for key customers. Denise would have to travel occasionally, servicing customers. Although Roger was not overjoyed by this, he agreed to cooperate since they had relatives nearby to help care for their child.

At first, Denise juggled her responsibilities well. She was proud of the way she could shift her schedule to make room for both her family and her career. But as Denise began enjoying her newfound freedom away from home, she soon became caught up in the "fun" lifestyle that went on after business hours. She thoroughly enjoyed going to the "in" night spots whenever she had to spend the night out of town. In fact, she enjoyed it so much that she started going to the hometown night spots rather than always rushing straight home from work like she used to. In this situation, it wasn't long until Denise became emotionally involved with another man. Since her schedule was flexible, she found it easy to allow an affair to develop, which is what happened.

One weekend, Denise broke the worst news to Roger that he had ever heard. She told him she was pregnant and that he was not the father. Roger had suspected that she might be interested in other men because their sex life had been waning. But this news caught him totally by surprise. She told him this didn't really matter because she had lost her feelings for him anyway. Soon after this news broke, Denise left home.

Roger was stunned. He didn't know what he was supposed to do. He kept asking: "How could this happen to me?" He felt like his life was a steamy soap opera script. Roger spent days in depression and agony. He was sure his life was ruined. He was embarrassed to face his friends and acquaintances. And worse, he was left with the haunting knowledge that he had a hand in his wife's problems since he knew that he had not been the most responsible husband in recent months.

About a week after Denise's departure, the situation took a turn for the worse. Roger learned that his wife had chosen to abort the child. This went totally against his convictions. He was dumbfounded, and again didn't know how to respond. He felt rage, loneliness, disillusionment, and pity all at the same time. Virtually all of his friends recommended divorce. Yet Roger felt that divorce was not necessarily the solution he wanted. Technically, he knew divorce was a live option since fornication was involved. But instead of immediately opting for this solution, he called Denise and set up a time for a discussion. In the intervening time, he spent hours in prayer seeking God's guidance.

During their meeting, tension hung heavily in the air. Denise knew that she had violated her most sacred principles and she found it difficult to look at Roger directly. Roger wanted to shout in anger but he knew it would serve no purpose. So he began to talk. He talked gently. He told his wife of the tremendous empty feeling he couldn't shake. He explained that he realized she was not the only person at fault. He knew that if he had been more responsive to the signs she had given, he would have detected her disinterest in the marriage. He explained how they had wandered from their original "team" commitment to each other and how, as a result, their marriage had slipped through their fingers. He reminded her of how they both had been selfishly tuned in to their own separate worlds.

Then Roger gave Denise the surprise of her life. He asked her to come home and remain his wife. He told her he forgave her of the wrongs she had done. He wanted to renew the commitment they had made twelve years earlier. He wanted to prove to her that he could be the husband she needed.

This was the last thing Denise expected from her husband. She had met with him expecting to hear him scream and yell. She fully expected to be divorced. She assumed that was what she deserved. She was ashamed that their original commitment had been shattered. She assumed their marriage was beyond repair. She was skeptical of Roger's invitation because she didn't think it would be humanly possible to restore love to their relationship. But since they had nothing to lose, she accepted his invitation.

The truth is, it was *not* humanly possible for Roger to rekindle his love for Denise. Privately, he admitted that his old feelings were not there. But he had made the decision to give his marriage to the Lord. First, he would concentrate on simply winning her back. He would patiently supply her with the support and understanding she needed. He decided he would concern himself with his feelings later. He knew that if he gave his actions over to God, He would eventually supply the emotions that had been so sorely bruised.

As you can imagine, it took a long time for Roger and Denise to get their marriage back on track. There were many times when both felt like giving up because they felt the odds were stacked against them. But they persisted, with Roger assuming the leadership.

Roger found that by choosing to do so, he could be more attentive to his wife's moods. He spent time with her at the end of the day. He put his arms around her when she looked tired or discouraged. He shared his feelings and beliefs with her like he had done when they had first become acquainted. He became the husband that Denise needed. He had resolved that he would live a life that typified a Christ-like love and nothing would stop him in his efforts.

In time, Denise responded. She was overwhelmed by the idea that Roger would love her after all that had happened. Because she knew that Roger didn't have to take her back with such forgiveness, she was impressed all the more with his efforts. As she realized the sincerity of his actions, she responded with her own demonstrations of tenderness and sensitivity. She felt special to him because they had gone to the depths of marital despair and Roger still wanted her.

Roger's decision was suprahuman. It was far and beyond human strength. The human decision would have been to discard the relationship and try again with someone else. But in their tribulation, Roger saw an opportunity to bring to their relationship a depth they had never known. In the beginning of their reconciliation, he had no idea whether or not his efforts would pay off. But that wasn't his primary concern. Roger only wanted to do what he thought would bring glory to God. He had set his feelings aside and, with God's help, stayed with his decision.

Many Rogers and Denises in this world assume that their broken relationship is beyond the point of return. Yet there still is hope for these people. Agape love knows no boundaries. No matter how great the obstacles, love can, with God's help, be summoned into one's life by a persistent exercising of the will. Whereas the other types of love come and go, agape love is permanent, if your mind and heart will let it be.

Love Is a Choice

Our culture places such heavy emphasis on the feeling aspect of love that it is hard to perceive of love any other way. But more than just a feeling, love is a choice. It is a way of life. This doesn't mean there is no feeling in love. (It would be naive to say that.) It does mean that love is something more than an emotional high you just fall in and out of. Look to the Bible's definition of love and you will find *action* rather than *feeling* words to describe it.

Love is patient, love is kind. It does not envy, it does not boast,
it is not proud. It is not rude, it is not self-seeking, it is not easily
angered, it keeps no record of wrongs. Love does not delight in
evil but rejoices with the truth. It always protects, always trusts,
always hopes, always perseveres (I Cor. 13:4-7).

When you understand love as a choice, it is then possible for
you to decide to adopt any one of the four styles of love described
in this chapter. Even if your feelings are not exactly where you
want them to be, love can still be demonstrated. This doesn't mean
that you are supposed to repress and deny other feelings. For
example, you may feel anger or loneliness. But those feelings don't
have to push love out. You can demonstrate love in spite of your
other feelings. You can determine your emotions, including love,
by the decisions you make.

Many people don't like to think of love as a choice. They feel
cheated if they don't have a persistent "high" that they assume is
the epitome of love. People who feel this way are usually self-
centered. That is, they are thinking more in terms of what they
will receive rather than what they will give. Even when these
people do get around to giving love, they usually have the ulterior
motive of wanting something in return.

More mature individuals realize that when love is freely given
by choice, the feelings will follow. Such people are not worried
about what they will receive. They already experience warm feelings because of their giving nature. They already feel the inherent
reward that comes from choosing love as a way of life. They experience the warm inner glow that follows any act of unselfish-
ness. There is a calm confidence in these people because they
know that giving is contagious.

People Love Differently

Many spouses will complain that their mates just don't love
them like they are supposed to. They point a finger at the "bad"
spouse and demand that the mate learn to be a better lover. These
people may have valid complaints. Some spouses really are lousy
at showing love. But more often, the complainers are being insen-
sitive in their complaints. What they actually are thinking is: "You're

not loving me the way I want you to love me." This changes the picture.

We all have visions of the ideal mate. We all want to be treated like kings and queens in our own homes. But the truth is, we all know that no mate is perfect. This may mean that your mate will not love you in quite the royal way you expect. But don't despair. Don't discount your spouse's efforts. Even though you may have something better in mind, you can still accept your spouse's way of love, imperfect though it may be. You can learn to go with what you've got.

Case Study: Expressing Love

Shirley complained that her husband, Mark, was not romantic enough. She wanted him to talk to her more. And she wanted him to "fuss over her" more than he did. Mark was a reserved man who was seldom overly expressive. But this didn't mean he didn't love his wife. He thought he was being loving when he listened as Shirley told about her day's activities. He thought he was being loving when he took her to the movies. He assumed he was loving when he came straight home from work so the family could eat dinner together. In other words, Mark and Shirley loved each other. But they had different ways to express their love.

When Shirley became insistent toward Mark in her conversations, Mark withdrew. So she learned the wisdom of gently making suggestions without pulling. Although Mark never did completely show his love to Shirley in the way she would have liked, she learned to look for his individual signals that indicated love was really there.

There is no best way to show love. This is because all people are different. It would be futile to try to make each mate follow a specific formula. If your mate is not loving you in exactly the way you want, there still is hope. Love still can exist.

Couples working for a good marriage will want to be sure their spouse is not left "out in the dark" wondering whether or not he or she is loved. Here are some guidelines to help your mate be aware of your love.

1. Remind your mate of your love and appreciation daily.
2. Tell your spouse *why* you appreciate the things he or she does.
3. Tell your spouse what makes you feel secure.

4. Set aside regular times when the two of you can get away from daily pressures. Go out on dates or take walks together.
5. Take on yourself the challenge to create a pleasant atmosphere in your home.
6. Do unexpected favors for your spouse. And don't worry about getting a reward in return.
7. Notice when your mate is trying hard to do right things. Pay compliments regularly.
8. When your partner is not in a loving mood, try even harder to be understanding.
9. Ask your spouse to give you feedback regarding your strengths and weaknesses.
10. Let your spouse know you don't expect perfection. Communicate an attitude of unconditional love.

Make God Your First Love

The reason some marriages have a disappointing love pattern is because each partner puts all his/her hopes and security into the mate. God takes second place. In some marriages, the love received from one's spouse is more important than the love received from God. Such couples worry so much about the ups and downs in their marital love life that they fail to claim the security provided by God.

The Bible teaches us that we are best able to experience real love in interpersonal relationships after we have experienced the love of God. We are able to love each other only because God first loved us (Read I John 4:19). We know that God is the creator of love. He is love personified. This means that we are going to be fully capable of loving each other after we enter into His love. The more we appreciate the love of God, the more we can make love a way of life.

Once you experience the union between yourself and God, His love becomes your love. His will becomes your will. Instead of putting your emotional life into the hands of your mate, you put it into the hands of a perfect God. Agape love becomes the dominant style of love in your life and the other three styles of love become more complete.

Once your pattern of love is established on the firm foundation of God's love, you will notice a significant decrease in the amount of pushing and pulling between you and your mate. Love that is a way of life seeks to avoid petty squabbling. It avoids the ups and downs that are a part of power struggles. Rather, it seeks to establish the flexibility, acceptance, and open communication that are a part of a give-and-take marriage.

part three

Knowledge that Leads to Action

12

Why Marriage?

Why do men and women want to be married in the first place? This question forces us to examine our own philosophy about the function of marriage, and that's good. For the answer, we need to look at our beginnings so graphically portrayed in the first two chapters of Genesis. God decided to create the heavens and the earth. That was an awesome decision, and pictures for us the greatness and might of God the Creator. Next came man (mankind). Man: the only creature created in the image of God. That is overwhelming! God created us as the pinnacle of all living things. That is overpowering!

Try to imagine what Adam's first days on earth must have been like. He may have spent hours each day wandering, soaking in the lush beauty around him. He got acquainted with the various plants and animals, and named them. He examined this new home at leisure and knew no fear, or hunger, or pain because his was a perfect world! Surely he must have shouted for the pure joy of fresh, unsullied life presented to him by God.

But God wanted even more for Adam. He never wanted Adam to be lonely, so He decided to give Adam a companion, a suitable helper (Gen. 2:18). This would bring completeness to Adam. God wanted Adam to share with a partner the joys of living. So out of God's love for Adam, Eve was created. She was the perfect complement to Adam, both emotionally and physically. And there in the Garden of Eden, the first wedding was performed by God Himself. God knew that Adam and Eve's open expressions of love to each other would prepare them to grasp spiritually and mentally His love toward them. The bond between husband and wife sym-

bolized the bond between God and His children. The creation of
Adam and Eve was part of God's perfect plan for our lives.

Haven from Loneliness: Sort of

Why do we pursue marriage? To answer our original question,
we get married to avoid loneliness. Marriage symbolizes the union
between God and man. Marriage was given to manifest in a tan-
gible, human experience the love of God. Marriage is God's gift of
love to us.

But skeptics remind us that some partners actually feel lonelier
than ever once they are married. They acknowledge the perfection
of the original marriage, but point to the sin-tarnished marriages
that have followed. They direct us to couples who have such a
difficult relationship that they have become totally disillusioned
with love.

These pessimistic commentaries on marriage are not entirely
wrong. Many of today's marriages are not what God originally
intended them to be. The original marriage (before sin) was different from marriage today. For example, Adam and Eve, before
sin, had the perfect ability to fulfill completely each other's emotional and physical needs. Each gave and received love fully. They
didn't fuss and fume over petty issues. They were able to talk
openly about anything. Their sex life was stimulating and proper.
Together they experienced life in the fullest sense.

No couple today knows this kind of perfect love. We all have
moments in our relationship when we feel "out of it." We all know
disappointments. We sometimes question the wisdom of God. We
question our mates. We question ourselves. Some couples decide
to quit trying. Why? What has happened since that first wedding?

Enter Sin—Enter Loneliness

Adam and Eve enjoyed perfection in their garden home. But at
some point in their lives (we don't know exactly when) something
snapped. God gave this first couple the capacity to make choices.
He gave them a will. And for a while, Adam and Eve made God's
will their will. But the day came when first Eve and then Adam
decided to test God. They used their God-given will and deliber-

ately chose to disobey His commandment. (Read Gen. 3:1-8 for an account of this.)

Once Adam and Eve chose to disobey God, bringing a pattern of sin into the world, three things happened. (1) A gulf opened between themselves and God. They no longer enjoyed perfect fellowship with God because they had dared to try to place themselves above Him. (2) A gulf opened up between Adam and Eve. Eve had deceived Adam, and a lack of trust developed between them. They no longer experienced the full sense of camaraderie they once had. Instead, each felt the need to hide and cover up. (3) A sense of shame and guilt enveloped both of them. Each became aware that they were sinners. A feeling of defensiveness was a natural outgrowth of this. Separation was born in two most vital relationships: with God and mate. A feeling of displeasure with self was engrained. In short, Adam and Eve began to feel the loneliness marriage was meant to dissipate.

God's original plan for marriage had been sabotaged by man's choice. So instead of enjoying a haven from loneliness, Adam and Eve actually created a feeling of distance. Separateness became a continuing part of their lives. No longer did they have the euphoria. Their relationship lost some meaningfulness. They were forced to contend with those gaps that are such a threat to marital relations.

In spite of best efforts to the contrary, marriages today follow the pattern established by Adam and Eve's fall into sin. No marriage now is going to completely fulfill a person's emotional, physical, or spiritual needs. We can even assume that every marital union will experience times of separateness. Gaps exist even in the best of marriages. What God originally gave mankind as an expression of love is now stained because of human sin. This fact causes some people to be overly pessimistic.

But are we doomed to unsatisfactory marriages just because we are not perfect? Is there no reason to try? Is there no reason for optimism? Let's examine loneliness to find some answers.

Separate, but Not Alone

We all have times of distance in our relationships. This is a fact of life. But gaps can be closed, and you can use your skills to close the gap. That is what a give-and-take marriage is designed to do! You are not doomed. For just as imperfection comes by choice, so also improvement comes by choosing to strive for it. Although you will never achieve perfection, you can still choose to work toward it.

Let's go back to our example of Adam and Eve. God knew that because our "earthly parents" had sinned, they would pass on this imperfection to their descendants. One evidence of this flaw surfaced as the earth was peopled, and those people began to take their marriage vows less and less seriously. They ignored God's plan for marital intimacy, and chose other directions. Loving actions were rejected in favor of the "me-first" philosophy. Other people went further, they engaged in intimacy with more than one sexual partner. Some perverts, in the hardness of their hearts, became intimate with members of their own sex. God's plan for their lives no longer concerned them. They lived in defiance of Him.

Divorce eventually became an option. People looked for excuses to break their wedding vows. God gave the laws of divorce because the hearts of many had hardened toward Him. But human views regarding marriage and divorce became liberal and self-indulgent. Marriage lost its original sacred position.

This low opinion of marriage infected other parts of people's lives. Commitments (to God, to people) were taken less seriously. Mutual sharing and loving died a slow death. Distrust and deceit became a part of life. The overall quality of life sunk to surprisingly low levels for those who spurned God's direction for their lives.

But marriage suffered the most. As the ultimate in human relationships, it had the most to lose.

A change was desperately needed. God was not willing to abandon His people despite their tendency to disobey. So rather than dismiss the human race wholesale, He made a provision to restore people to their original standing. He kept the options open for us to return to a right way of living. This is where Jesus Christ entered the stream of history.

Jesus Christ is God's provision to bring humans back into a right relationship with Him. Christ accepted the punishment for our defiance of God, and rebuilt the bridge between God and man. When we accept Christ as our salvation, we become united to Jesus and able to be presented once again before God as members of His kingdom. Christ is the bridegroom, we the believers are the bride. We become newly created when we are in Him.

When our nature is restored through Christ's atonement, the flaws in our personality can be rebuilt. Likewise, the gaps (the loneliness) in human relations can be closed. By following Christ's living example as the perfect bridegroom, we can bring wholeness to our relationships. Rather than dwelling on the sinful, imperfect elements in marriage, we can go back to God's original concept of marriage. Through Christ we are enabled to live life the way God wanted Adam and Eve to live it. We can accept marriage as a glorious gift from God. We draw our marriage plan from the words of Jesus who reiterated God's original concept for marriage: "What therefore God has joined together, let no man separate" (Mark 10:9).

Shoot for the Stars, but Relax

I once talked with a man about God's plan for marriage. We discussed at length the tendency for Christians to "shoot for the stars." That is, as Christians we know the highest truths and we want to pursue them. But while we talked, this man reminded himself he wasn't always fully tuned in to his Christian goals. Like it or not, he still felt there were gaps in his marriage. He felt discouraged when he fell short of his lofty ideals. He said: "If I am supposed to be shooting for the stars, I feel like I am way off

target. I'm only hitting the moon!" His words reflect the frustration
of one who knows the ideals of marriage but feels inept at the
task.

In our Christian lives, as God's new creation, we will want to
strive for ideals. We will want to regain the position of Adam and
Eve before the Fall. We will want to give each other enough love
to ward off lonely feelings. But what about the Christian who *is*
trying to live right, but persistently falls short? Is it ever okay to
just give up and go on to something else? How far is far enough?

You will encounter a paradox when you seek to realize God's
original intention for your marriage. That is, rather than being
threatened by the loneliness that can occur in any union, you can
accept that loneliness exists and go from there. You must accept
loneliness before you can beat it. The more threatened you are by
it, the more it will overwhelm you. The more calmly you handle
it, the less it will bother you.

This illustration may help. Suppose you are in a friend's yard,
and a little puppy comes running toward you. It is excited and
begins to bark and jump on you. What happens if you also get
jumpy and run to try to get away from the puppy? Naturally, it
becomes even *more* excited and increases its activity. But if you
reach down and gently rub the dog, it calms down immediately.
By acting in a confident, composed manner, you easily keep the
situation under control.

Apply this idea to handling separateness in your marital relationship. If you become anxious, fidgety, and excited when gaps
appear in your marriage, they will only get worse. But if you rationally accept imperfections that occur, and are not threatened
by your mutual mistakes, your problems will be minimized and
decrease.

Your confidence can be based on the assurance that comes from
knowing you are attempting to live your life according to God's
original plan. You know that it can be rewarding. You may never
have all the perfect moments you desire, but consistent efforts
will bring you closer to the ideal.

I John 4:12 reads: "If we love one another, God abides in us, and
His love is perfected in us." This sums up God's original design
for our lives. Our love for one another makes it possible for us to

know God. This is what He had in mind when He created Adam and Eve. "Perfected" in this passage means "having fulfilled the purpose for which God made you." That doesn't sound so hard, does it? In fact, it is more attainable than you may have guessed.

As a husband or wife who is trying to steer away from the push-pull pattern, your challenge is to find your purpose and pursue it. This leads us directly into the next chapter.

Finding Your Purpose

In the West Texas prairie, tumbleweeds seem to be everywhere. Incessant winds easily snap these fragile balls of brush from their weak root systems, freeing the plants to blow with the breezes. A natural function is fulfilled as plant seeds scatter, later to continue the life cycle.

Tumbleweeds bouncing along with the wind furnish us with a picture of rootlessness so prevalent in modern human society. Some people float from one job to another; others seem unable to maintain close friendships and lack intimacy even with family members. Thousands are blown away from reality through drugs or alcohol.

The area hurt most by the "tumbleweed pattern" is marriage. Far too many couples drift aimlessly through dating and courtship and into marriage without serious planning or thoughtful evaluation. They are swept along on the current of their emotions, and finally decide to marry simply because they "feel" right for each other. Or, it's the customary thing to do: their friends are doing it; their relatives have done it. But when they're married, they don't know exactly what to do with feelings that seem to sway back and forth. Love comes and goes. One day they feel committed, but the next day they're ready to give up. They look for a foundation and find none in which to anchor their relationship. The lack of any strong sense of purpose quickly pushes such couples into destructive push-pull patterns.

Even thoughtful, mature young men and women may find their marital dreams too quickly shattered because they do not realize that in the Bible God provides clear guidelines for marriage partners. The Creator who designed marriage also furnishes directives for discovering and fulfilling a fundamental sense of purpose through marriage and family life.

The good news we will explore in this chapter is that couples can find a sense of purpose in marriage. A foundation can be laid. As we look to God's Word we will find the ingredients necessary to keep us on course.

Marriage as a Merger

The first two chapters of Genesis give the inspired account of the creation of the first couple.

> Then God said, "Let Us make man in Our image, according to Our likeness; and let them rule over the birds of the sky and over the cattle and over all the earth, and over every creeping thing that creeps on the earth."
> And God created man in His own image, in the image of God He created him; male and female He created them (Gen. 1:26,27).

Adam was created first (Gen. 2:7) and then Eve (Gen. 2:22). God placed this couple in an ideal, sinless environment: the Garden of Eden. Theirs was a union of purpose, wills, and spirit. Neither functioned as an isolated individual. They came together in body and soul, which gave wholeness to them both. Each completed the other and fulfilled the divine purpose of their creation: to glorify God.

The second chapter of Genesis gives a "zoom lens" account of the overview of creation in chapter one, detailing the creation of the first man.

> Then the Lord God formed man of dust from the ground, and breathed into his nostrils the breath of life, and man became a living being (Gen. 2:7).

Although Adam had fellowship with God and found companionship among the animals, he had psychological and interpersonal needs that only another human being could fill. God knew this and provided a woman for him.

As the chapter unfolds, woman is created, and in woman, Adam discovers a suitable helper uniquely able to complete and complement him in every way. They were brought together as husband and wife by God Himself.

The woman was created from man and created for him, as a completer. But the entrance of sin — Adam and Eve's disobedience of God's command — disrupted God's divine purpose for creation and for marriage. Harmony gave way to selfishness. The earlier idyllic love and mutual respect that Adam and Eve enjoyed together was diminished by exploitation and resentment. The marred relationship was passed on to the human race for all time.

But God, in love, prescribed a structure for the human family. He gave clear guidelines whereby men and women, although imperfect, can build marriages and homes that are a source of joy, love, and companionship. God intended marriage to be an institution of mutual love and interdependence.

> However, in the Lord, neither is woman independent of man nor is man independent of woman. For as the woman originates from the man, so also the man has his birth through the woman; and all things originate from God (II Cor. 11:11, 12).

Each mate has unique purpose and function. And both must do their part if wholeness is to be restored to marriage. Let's look first at biblical guidelines for the husband.

God's Purpose for Husbands

The first two chapters of Genesis give us a clear picture of creation, including God's first human creation — Adam (man).

Man was expected to be a caretaker or governor of God's created works (see Gen. 1:26, 28, 29 and Chapter 2:5, 20). Adam was given initial authority and responsibility, and together with Eve they were assigned to care for the newly-created earth. God had thoroughly equipped Adam for his responsibilities.

To further understand God's purpose for husbands, let's use this illustration. On a doubles tennis team, one person serves as captain. The captain takes initiative to map out strategy. He represents the team in a contest. In doing so, however, he draws from the strengths of his partner. He knows that to win, they must work together. So everything he does takes into consideration their combined strengths and weaknesses. As team captain, his

"I'll handle the net shots on my side. You handle the net shots on your side and *all* of the lobs on both sides."

primary responsibility is to work for cooperation in a coordinated effort. So it is with husbands. A husband is the God-assigned leader in a marriage who is to be mindful of the needs of his teammate. With this in mind, let's look at God's directions for husbands and how they can give a husband a deep sense of purpose.

1. Husbands are directed to be sacrificial.

Husbands, love your wives, just as Christ also loved the church and gave Himself up for her (Eph. 5:25).

Christ, the bridegroom, loved His bride (the church) and gave Himself up for her. Husbands, this means that Jesus has set the standard and you are urged to "give yourself up" for your wife. Christ sacrificed His very life for the church's gain. He set His will aside and voluntarily gave Himself up.

Can a husband set aside his own desires and live for the good of his wife? It is a challenge. It's tough. It calls for a self-sacrificing spirit. In a practical sense, this means husbands should look for ways to bring harmony into the marriage. Husbands, you need to be so committed to loving your wife in the agape manner that you actively search for ways to sacrifice your desires for hers in favor of marital unity. That is hard and against natural impulses, but the end results are well worth the effort.

2. Husbands are to care for their wives as they care for themselves.

So husbands ought also to love their own wives as their own bodies. He who loves his own wife loves himself; for no one ever hated his own flesh, but nourishes and cherishes it, just as Christ also does the church, because we are members of His body (Eph. 5:28-29).

Most men have a desire to look good, feel good, even "smell" good. It's natural. It's good. Caring for our bodies is necessary for our sense of well-being. In addition, a man also knows he will need spiritual and emotional care. He knows how laughter will sometimes meet his need. Sometimes he will need people, and other times he will need silence. He is generally tuned in to the kind of care he needs.

And just as a man cares for himself he should minister to the needs of his wife, whether the needs are material, spiritual, or emotional.

3. A husband is to be understanding.

You husbands likewise, live with your wives in an understanding way, as with a weaker vessel, since she is a woman; and grant her honor as a fellow-heir of grace of life, so that your prayers may not be hindered (I Peter 3:7).

This verse is speaking of the difference in psychological natures of men and women. The implication is for men to recognize and respect the innate sensitivity of women as opposed to men whose nature tends to exhibit itself in a more rugged manner. Understand that your wife may think and feel differently than you do because of her very nature. Her reasoning may not always coincide with yours. But that doesn't mean she is automatically wrong. It does mean that she may view something from her unique feminine perspective. Rather than imposing your nature on her, make allowances for the areas of contrast, and respond in an understanding way.

4. A husband is to grant honor to his wife.

... and grant her honor as a fellow-heir of grace of life, so that your prayers may not be hindered (I Peter 3:7).

Let's go back to a point made earlier. That is, God gave woman to man. Adam was the recipient of a very special creation of God. Your wife is special also. She is to receive top billing in your life. She is the one you have chosen to spend your life with, and when you honor her you are saying in essence to the world, "My wife is very special. She is my chosen one." Husbands, the more you determine to live according to God's purposes, the more satisfaction it will bring to you and your wife.

God's Purpose for Wives

In the beginning Adam was alone, and needed another human to complement and correspond to him. God met this need in the creation of woman who was in every way a suitable helper. She was all Adam's nature demanded for completion: physically, spiritually, emotionally, intellectually, and socially. Man's need and woman's ability to meet that need formulated the foundation for a unique, one-flesh relationship.

The New Testament instructions we'll discuss find their taproots in creation, and are given for the purpose of helping women rediscover and restore the original joy intended for marriage. Let's look at God's directives for women:

1. A wife is to be submissive.

Wives, be subject unto your own husbands as to the Lord. For the husband is the head of the wife, as Christ also is the head of the church, He himself being the Savior of the body (Eph. 5:22,23).

In other words, a wife should acknowledge and yield to the authority of her husband. The reasons for such submission are given in verse 23.

This is one of several passages in the New Testament which strongly urge the wife to develop an attitude of trust in and deference to the final authority of her husband. Let me quickly add that many people confuse submission with submersion. Submission does not mean that a wife is to voice no opinions of her own and have no input in decision-making.

Because woman was created to complete and complement her husband, she must, necessarily be a contributing member of the team. If a wife "closets" all her ideas and opinions under the cloak of submission, she cannot either complement or complete her husband. She will, in fact, rob her husband of key information he needs to make wise decisions. She will also deprive herself of the rewards of cooperative teamwork. Many decisions in marriage are the final outcome of two sets of complementary insights, and for a wife to withhold her perspective and input under the guise of being submissive is to shortchange the marriage and misunderstand Scripture.

When a wife chooses to be submissive to her husband, it is a self-denying act of Christ-like love, and is given from a position of spiritual strength. It is a conscious decision to defer to a husband's authority, and a decisive act of deference exhibiting a spirit controlled and directed by God. This kind of spirit contributes immensely to an overall harmony in marriage, and clearly demonstrates a desire to obey God. By living in submission to her husband, the wife is recognizing that marriage requires team effort.

Submission is not passivity, but rather an active, voluntary decision made in obedience to God. An attitude of submission can be present even if the wife has a social, spiritual, or economic advantage over her husband. His headship exists regardless of the occupation or social standing of either spouse.

In this area, we need to emphasize that a wife owes submission to God first and foremost (Acts 5:29). God's Word is the only pure standard of conduct, and the wife's conduct should conform to God's commands. If a husband's desires conflict with God's commands, particularly in the area of moral decisions, a wife's obedience is to God.

When the husband obeys God's commands, the wife suffers no hardship from her submission to him. Her attitude, in fact, will tend to evoke a loving response from her husband, and make it easier for him to obey God. But, if he does not respond in love, the wife will find it personally unprofitable to be disobedient to God's Word. A wife's submission to her husband is rooted in submission to a loving God and her obedience will be rewarded by Him. She is responsible as an individual to obey God.

This is not to say a wife will never desire to control and manipulate her husband, but rather that she does not let that desire determine her actions. A wife who wrests control from her husband does so at the risk of undermining the happiness and fulfillment that is possible when mates obey God.

2. A wife is to respect her husband.

> ... and let the wife see that she respects her husband (Eph. 5:33).

Respect, like submission, is also a decision. To respect your husband carries with it the thought of valuing him the way God values him. Look for the best in him, and make a practice of reinforcing his strengths. This can be done in a number of ways. Support the work he is involved in. Do all you can to help him succeed. Dwell on his good traits and pay him sincere compliments. Seek his advice about decisions. Thank him regularly for the thoughtful things he does for you. Make him feel special in ways only you can.

Showing respect to your mate really helps you and the rest of your family. A man who feels valued by his wife will instinctively value his wife more. But even if he doesn't, you still win! Generally, you will enjoy much greater sense of personal peace when you are looking for the best in your mate.

3. Wives are to be consistent in Christ-like behavior.

> In the same way, you wives, be submissive to your own husbands so that even if any of them are disobedient to the word, they may be won without a word by the behavior of their wives, as they observe your chaste and respectful behavior (I Peter 3:1,2).

A wife with consistent, Christ-like behavior wields a powerful influence for good on even the most wayward, unstable marriage. Behavior says much more than words, and according to the passage above, chaste, respectful behavior in a wife can win a husband over to a personal trust in Christ. Accept the challenge to be a steady force in your marital union. Don't give in to the tumbleweed pattern but, rather, hold firmly to the purpose for which God has called you. Be a consistent, godly, completer for your husband.

4. Wives are to be chaste (I Peter 3:2). Chaste is an old-fashioned word in today's vocabulary. Its common usage denotes an undefiled meaning. Chaste also refers to a pure heart. If you are a pure, chaste wife, you will live cleanly. And you won't be a person riddled by the kinds of guilt that detract from your effectiveness as a wife.

As a pure wife, you will aim to keep yourself free from sinful error. You will not be given to carousing and frivolity. Instead, you will draw pleasure from creating a clean emotional atmosphere in your home. In a world filled with debauchery and immorality, you can be a much-needed breath of fresh air.

5. Wives are to be quiet and gentle.

And let not your adornment be merely external — braiding the hair, and wearing gold jewelry, and putting on dresses; but let it be the hidden person of the heart, with the imperishable quality of a gentle and quiet spirit, which is precious in the sight of God. For in this way in former times the holy woman also, who hoped in God, used to adorn themselves, being submissive to their own husbands (I Peter 3:3-5).

The above verses are not a picture of the woman who likes to draw attention to herself, one who may dress provocatively, or tries to be the center of attention wherever she is; one whose main interest is focused on herself, who is loyal first and foremost to "me," who considers others as second in line.

If you are working to create an atmosphere of give and take in your marriage, bold, flashy behavior won't work. The best results come from exhibiting a gentle nature. A gentle nature doesn't mean that you should shuffle around the house with lowered head and sealed lips. It means that you will do kind things your husband enjoys without drawing attention to yourself. You will behave in a gentle way that has a soothing effect on your relationship. You will seek to minimize anger and maximize tenderness. As a result, you will build temperance and courtesy into your marriage.

The five actions we have discussed cause some interesting reactions in both husbands and wives: (1) You will create a receptive heart in your husband. He will increasingly be drawn to you. (2) You will generate a personal sense of contentment and increase your self-esteem and worth. (3) You will bring honor to God. By being the wife God wants you to be, your witness for Him increases and you will be living in His glory.

Guaranteed Reward

As you strive to live according to your calling as a husband or wife, you will be guaranteed a reward. I Peter 3:9 says "For you were called for the very purpose that you might inherit a blessing." God created the institution of marriage because He knew what blessing a life of marital harmony is. From the very beginning He has wished for us nothing but the best. The provision of marriage is a reflection of His love.

Let's focus on one final thought. Cooperation in your joint endeavor is an invaluable ally. The wife's task is made easier by a husband who works hard to be the right kind of husband. And likewise, the husband's work is easier when the wife holds up her end of the relationship. The ideal is husbands and wives both on the same side, working for the same goal.

But, you may ask: "What if my spouse isn't working as hard as I am?" Don't let that stop you. You may never know how much of an impact your loving efforts can have on your mate. But even if you don't receive what you want, you can still find motivation to live according to your purpose. After all, you can make your efforts knowing that ultimately you will please God.

14

Seeing Marriage Through Divorce

One of the best ways to pursue the give-and-take pattern in marriage is to come to grips with your beliefs about divorce. This process will clarify what you want to achieve in marriage. Whatever your conviction about the rightness or wrongness of divorce, that belief influences your actions, and needs to be fully understood.

Attitudes toward divorce today tend to fall into one of two categories: (1) Couples should remain married until death. Divorce is an option only in the case of fornication, according to the teaching of Christ (Matt. 5:31-32). (2) Divorce is unfortunate, but if it seems "inevitable," get it over with and get on with the business of life.

If marriages are to be preserved, the second point of view is risky, to say the least. All Christian couples need a strong foundational belief about divorce that follows biblical guidelines. A lax philosophy, as opposed to Christian teachings, will produce an easy-come/easy-go attitude toward marriage. Yet it's not enough for a couple to state they don't believe in divorce only because that's what the Bible teaches. If a couple's only reason for staying married is to preserve a biblical rule, then bitterness toward God and the Bible is likely to result. It is important for couples to know why divorce is discouraged. This understanding will give depth and quality to beliefs, and they become much more than mere rules you must follow.

A History of Divorce

Jesus taught:

> It has been said, Whoever shall put away his wife let him give her
> a writing of divorcement. But I say to you, that whoever shall put
> away his wife, except for the cause of fornication, causes her to
> commit adultery, and whoever shall marry her that is divorced
> commits adultery (Matt. 5:31-32).

Jesus was speaking these words to people who seemed to take
delight in arguing fine points of the Mosaic law. But in stating this
new law, Jesus was issuing a challenge. In essence He was communicating: "You seemed to be so worried about what the law
says regarding divorce, but why a divorce at all?" He was stressing
that a violation of God's sacred marriage vows was equally as
serious as infidelity.

Centuries earlier, in the time of Moses, the Jews had been given
permission to divorce. However, in giving this law, Moses certainly
had no intention of creating a flippant attitude toward marriage.
The law of divorce was a reluctant concession on God's part because of the hardness of the people's hearts (read Deut. 24:1-2).
Remember, God still wanted people to pursue His original goals
for marriage.

In the intervening years between the Old Testament law and
Jesus' words in the New Testament, some people abused the law
of divorce. Many men were dealing unreasonably with their wives.
In fact, some of the men were so harsh and demanding that they
would divorce their wives for petty reasons such as poor house-
keeping. All the while their chief concern was to keep the letter
of the law. The scribes and Pharisees would argue for hours about
how the decree of divorcement should be written. But they would
spend very little time considering why the decree should (or should
not) be given. Marriage had lost its original sanctity.

Chapter 4 of John's gospel records Jesus' encounter with the
woman at the well. She had been married five times and was then
living with a man out of wedlock. Sadly, hers was not an unheard
of situation! In the time of Jesus it was not even unusual for some

of the pious Pharisees to have had several marriages. As long as they felt they were living within the technicalities of the law, they did as they pleased. They didn't bother to grasp God's masterplan for their lives.

Therefore, Christ's restatement of the law of divorce was necessary. He recognized a flippant attitude toward marriage among even the most religious. His intent was to get the people to take their focus off legalistic battles regarding the technicalities of divorce, and to consider instead God's plan for their lives.

Current Struggles with the Issue of Divorce

When marital problems erupt, it is wise to consult the Bible for guidance. But in doing so, recognize the danger of adopting the same legalistic attitude that characterized the Pharisees of Jesus' day. Some people whose spouses have committed adultery feel it is required to get a divorce. Others will reason that although God does not like divorce, it is acceptable to get a divorce as long as they ask God's forgiveness. Technically, these people can make good arguments for their case. God does allow divorce in the case of infidelity. God is willing to forgive when we go against His plan for our lives. But that's not necessarily the point!

Jesus wasn't trying to create a new system of legalism when He stated His position on divorce. Rather than to create a new law, Jesus taught an internal sense of responsibility. He intended that we remember the permanency of marriage as a purposeful act symbolizing God's union with His people. He wanted to take His listeners back to the basics.

Therefore, instead of figuring out what we can get away with and still be in line with the Bible, we should seek to understand the implications behind the guidelines. In a growing marriage, partners will seek to bring dignity to their relationship in the manner intended by God. This helps lead the couple from the push-pull pattern to the give-and-take pattern.

Your feelings about divorce will directly influence your attitudes toward marriage. Most couples pursuing a give-and-take marriage will find that they are most satisfied when they avoid the extreme views about divorce. They will avoid the extreme that considers divorce a ready option because this view does little to bring a sense of security to the relationship. And they will avoid the other extreme declaring that couples must absolutely, positively never think about divorce. Rather, the partners will realize that they are responsible to make their personal choice, while recognizing that the best choice will be guided by a firm commitment to biblical guidelines.

Thus, a merely "legalistic" stance (keeping the rules simply for the sake of keeping the rules) on marriage and divorce is not necessary. People who grit their teeth and stay married just to follow the rules usually feel miserably stuck. In their efforts to tough it out "for the Lord," they ruin themselves and feel like phonies. (I call these people "gruesome twosomes.") These people need a change in mental focus. Rather than thinking "It looks like I've got nothing ahead of me but years of misery," they can take the attitude that says "In my struggles I am going to find new ways to be a better spouse and a better person." This attitude is far more successful than anything legalism can produce.

Case Study: Divorce Dilemma

Phil and Jean went through some very trying experiences before coming to grips with their philosophy toward divorce. They had married while they were still in college. Hindsight told them they were too immature to be married then. Nonetheless, it had happened. For the first two or three years they sincerely tried to make the most of their relationship. But the thought kept popping into their heads that they were not meant for each other. After going through much pushing and pulling, they decided to divorce. Though there was no infidelity involved, they reasoned that God didn't want them to live in disharmony all their lives. Surely He would understand their decision and forgive.

They were in no hurry to rush the legal paperwork along in the divorce proceedings. Consequently, their separation dragged on for a year before their case came to court. During that year of waiting, each had felt a sense of relief and a sense of discomfort. They felt relieved because they were not going home each night to constant arguing. But they were uncomfortable because each knew they were not living up to their Christian potential.

Each had spent long hours inwardly questioning their decision to divorce. Though they felt technically free to divorce, they were experiencing a lack of spiritual growth. When the day came that they were to stand in the courtroom for the final pronouncement of divorce, they looked at one another and shook their heads simultaneously. Tears were in their eyes as Phil questioned: "What on earth are we doing here?" At that moment they dismissed their lawyers and went home together, convinced that it was right to stay married.

Phil and Jean knew that they didn't *have to* stay married. But they decided they *would*. Their decision was not based on rules. They had set aside all the legalistic arguments and had considered marriage in the biblical context.

Their struggle with the decision to divorce was the springboard that helped Phil and Jean come to the decision to try to create a give-and-take marriage. Instead of falling victim to the constant bantering of their old push-pull pattern, they knew they wanted to have a meaningful relationship. They knew it would require effort from both of them. They prepared themselves mentally and emotionally to work on their marriage even if it would take years to reach the point of consistent mutual satisfaction.

When Divorce Becomes an Issue

Predictably enough, a couple deeply entrenched in a push-pull marriage will begin to think about divorce. But their marriage is not hopeless simply because they have entertained the notion of divorce. Not at all. Couples in even the most difficult marriages can experience increasing contentment. Discipline is the key to success. Even if only one partner is working to make the marriage work there is room for hope. These basic guidelines deserve attention when divorce becomes an issue.

1. View your undesirable circumstances as built-in opportunities for personal growth. It's easy to try to be a good spouse when things are going great. Almost anyone can do that. But the mark of real maturity comes when the pursuit of self-improvement continues in difficult circumstances. When divorce becomes an issue, couples are faced with the most disenchanting kind of rejection. Unwanted emotions such as anger, guilt, discouragement, depression, and loneliness creep in. But rather than "caving in" under

your experiences, you can commit yourself to learn from your mistakes. Examine yourself. Make new guidelines for your behavior. Consider this an opportunity to make some necessary changes.

2. Examine your expectations. People on the brink of divorce usually discover they have been expecting too much from their spouses. Their "want list" has been too long, and they have focused too heavily on what they think they should receive. Write down the expectations you have for your spouse. Be as honest and specific as you can be. When you finish, go back over your list and cross off ones you could live without. Then examine the remaining expectations and determine how you can use love as your guide as you retain those expectations. Then question yourself: Which is more important, your expectations for your spouse or your love for your spouse?

3. Look for new ways to show love. We all know that love involves your emotions. But more importantly, love involves your actions. You can choose to express love as a way of life even if your emotions at the moment are not tuned to love. You know your mate well enough to know what makes him/her happy. So look for ways to create a pleasant atmosphere. Even if your efforts are rejected at first, try again. Don't give up. If you have to prove your love to your spouse with the passing of time, do it.

4. Re-evaluate your relationship with God. The major reason spouses have problems that lead to divorce is a lack of focus on the love God has for them. A deep experience in your relationship with God will influence your relationship with people. God allows humans to experience difficulties, knowing that through those difficulties He can express His nature more clearly to them. Spend time in prayer. Spend time studying His word. Join a group of committed believers. You can find new purpose in your marriage as you experience the profound depth of God's love.

5. Commit yourself to take initiative in your efforts to bring change. When divorce becomes an issue, don't sit back and wait for your spouse to put the broken pieces back together. You can be the one to take initiative in creating the right kind of marriage atmosphere. If you wait for your spouse to make these moves, you will probably become a cynic. The knowledge that you are making the effort fosters hope.

As partners grow, they will allow themselves to look at all sides of any issue. Their information becomes rounded out, and their understanding increases. They can talk together about their thoughts on divorce. As they discuss an issue, they can better understand what they should plan to do to improve their marriage.

Remember, don't merely dismiss the entire topic of divorce by saying, "the Bible says we are not supposed to do it." Go beyond — go deeper. Learn *why* you believe the way you do.

15

Self-Image:
The Hub of the Wheel

Almost everything you do is a direct reflection of your self-image. That's a pretty strong statement. Yet it's true. Whatever you do or don't do says something about the way you feel about yourself.

Case Study: Low Self-Image

Lydia came to my office originally because she was suffering from depression. However, it did not take long for us to come to the conclusion that her root problem was her low self-image. Because she had always assumed that she could not measure up to the expectations of family and friends, she had taken a defeated view toward herself. As you would imagine, when she interacted with her husband she was defensive and insecure. Her poor marital situation contributed to her depression. She was caught in a terrible cycle.

However, in time, Lydia began recognizing that she did not have to continuously hold to the old thought that she was inadequate. We discussed at length how as an adult she had some positive thinking capacities that had been left untapped. As she began formulating a new pattern of thoughts about her sense of worth, she noticed that she was less prone to become bogged down in frustrating communication patterns. She learned the art of give-and-take toward all her relationships by objectively examining her own belief about herself.

Picture a wagon wheel with self-image as the hub. Your behavior and feelings are spokes extending from the hub. When your self-image is in good shape, it follows that your behaviors and feelings will be in line. Or, if your behaviors and feelings are going haywire, there is a problem at the hub, your self-image.

In your marriage whenever you find yourself in a pattern leading nowhere fast, there is a reason. Push-and-pull behaviors don't drop out of the sky. They begin inside you. If you tend to argue constantly, you do it because of your self-image. If it's difficult to speak up and share your feelings, that, too, has an inner source. Being moody, sensitive, hard-headed, or cold-hearted are all outward indications of trouble at the hub.

Some people may work tirelessly to make things seem right in their marriages. They may try to divert or change surface problems but discover that basic relationship problems are still on a collision course. Their relationship problems continue because they are dealing only with surface tensions, not the inner difficulty.

This illustration pinpoints the problem. A department store is having severe financial strains due to poor management practices. But instead of dealing with the heart of the matter, the president decides to redecorate the façade of the store and refurbish the showrooms inside. This completed, the store looks better, but the root problems remain. Why? Because the president didn't deal with the real problem. He focused only on the more superficial matters and in reality increased the difficulty.

In growing marriages, the real issue is the ego (self-image) of each spouse. Couples may work frantically to make things look right on the outside. But until the deepest issue is resolved, outside changes will only be temporary. It's what is on the inside that counts!

Barriers to a Positive Self-Image

Why do some people feel good about themselves naturally, while others have continued problems in loving themselves? There is usually no single answer to this question. Rather, a combination of factors contribute to self-image problems. Here are some reasons that help to explain why people may have a hard time properly loving themselves.

1. A person may have experienced unsatisfactory or insufficient parental love. We are all creatures of habit. And most of our habits

originated in childhood. For children, parental love is one of the most important needs. Young people formulate their feelings toward themselves based on their perception of their parents' love for them. Very often, parents can unintentionally express conditional love. They may seem to withhold love when the child does not live up to expectations. This could cause children to doubt themselves. If this continues for years, the habit can become deeply engrained.

A more painful variation of conditional love is practiced by parents who openly tell their children they are not okay. Countless numbers of children have been told plainly and often by parents that they were no good or they would never succeed. In moments of frustration, parents may say things they know they shouldn't. But the words once spoken, can never be recalled. Children on the receiving end of such messages may have a hard time feeling worthwhile later as adults.

"Fortunately, it's not your blood pressure or your stress level; it's your ego level."

2. A person may feel rejected by his/her spouse. Some people may enter marriage with self-images intact. But repeated rejections from a spouse can cause confidence to take a plunge. Next to parents, the marital partner is the most influential person in helping an adult sustain feelings of self-worth. This emphasizes the importance of the "giving" dimensions of love toward your mate. If that love is withdrawn, your mate loses part of the foundation for a healthy self-love. Worse, when derogatory, hateful words are used on a spouse, the result can be devastating.

3. A person may have been taught that self-love is wrong and that only conceited people love themselves. Self-love is equated with pride. Humility includes thinking about themselves negatively.

Such people fail to understand that self-love and humility can coexist! One element does not cancel out the other. There is a difference between being arrogant and feeling worthwhile. Although some teaching against self-love is well intended, it could cause a person to have a distorted view of the value God places on people.

4. A person may believe self-love is based on performance. Many people have a positive self-image only when they perform well. These people feel good about themselves when they can grade themselves with an A+. This is a easy habit to fall prey to, since Americans are frequently evaluated from the time they take their first steps until the day they die.

There is one major problem with a self-image based on performance: no one is perfect. No one can give a "winning performance" all the time. The self-image must have a more secure base than mere performance.

5. A person may allow others to exercise a god-like control over his/her self-image. Many individuals allow other people to be their "gods." They may pick out one or two significant persons and rely on them for feelings of worth. That significant person may be a spouse, a parent, a friend, or even a child. When that significant person treats them well or showers them with praise, all is well. But if the significant person rejects them, self-esteem melts away. The entire self-image rests on the opinion of this idolized person.

Push-pull marriage partners frequently are afflicted with this "idolized person" concept. When, for example, a wife relies so heavily on her husband for her emotional stability that she allows him to determine her feeling of worth, the marriage is headed for trouble. Why does such a wife spend so much energy trying to impose her will on her husband? She's looking for some predictability from him. She wants some praise, some guarantee that she has worth. She wants her idolized person or "god" to tell her again and again that she's doing well. Her fragile self-image needs constant reinforcement.

How to Have a Positive Self-Image

Explaining how to have a positive self-image is easy, but putting the how-to into practice is often difficult. That requires persistence. Rather than a "doing" exercise, it is a way of thinking. To

have a positive self-image, fix your thoughts on some unchange-
able truths that produce a positive self-image even when your
feelings don't cooperate.

Your entire self-image ultimately rests in your position before
God. Being the Creator, He is the only one who can bestow worth
on any individual. To focus on your position in Him, first get rid
of all other "gods." That is, recognize that your mate is not a god.
Your financial standing is not a "god" to give you worth. Your
achievements do not give you value. These are temporary, tran-
sient factors in your life. To base your self-image on them is "high
risk."

To develop a positive self-image, remember four basic facts.
Nothing can change the truth of these facts and they can become
a sure foundation for a solid self-image.

1. God loves you unconditionally. Because we experience so
much conditional love from people, it's easy to assume that God
does the same. In error, we think His love comes and goes. Human
love is unpredictable at best. That is, people tend to expect certain
standards to be met before they give their love. Some people are
stingy with love, others are more liberal. But the fact remains —
human love has limits. God's love does not have these limitations.

Contrast human love with love that has no conditions. It is
almost impossible to fully imagine love that keeps on flowing no
matter what the recipient does. This means that when you tell lies,
God still loves you (He is saddened, but His love continues). When
you fail to be a good spouse, the love is there. When you are lazy,
when you are obnoxious, or when you knowingly do wrong, God
still loves you. His love is unconditional and constant.

2. You are the object of God's infinite love. "For God so loved
the world, that He gave His only begotten son. ..." John 3:16 says
it all. His love for you as an individual resulted in the redemptive
death of Christ who willingly gave Himself as payment for your
personal sin. No one would lay down his life for something that
was worthless. The very worth of the sacrifice (the Son of God)
indicates the value placed on you.

3. You are the object of God's discipline. Discipline when properly administered, is a demonstration of care and concern. Admittedly, some parents do not always use discipline appropriately.

Yet the ultimate motivation behind proper discipline is love. Children who receive discipline do not always understand why it is given. Often years elapse before the discipline makes sense. Likewise, you sometimes may be confused about the discipline of God. But if you could view His discipline as a demonstration of fatherly love for you, His child, perhaps you, too, could learn to accept it as a gift.

You can gain a sense of security because you know that God cares enough for you to help you learn from your mistakes. In the process He allows you to experience the consequences of your mistakes. He allows you to wade through unpleasant struggles. He wants to motivate you to make improvements so you can experience the fullness of life in His will. Thankfully, God loves you and prizes you too much to simply let you make unbridled, sinful choices. As you turn to Him and accept His discipline you can gain a sense of worth, knowing He cares enough to discipline you.

4. You have a home waiting for you. One of the most awe-inspiring sections of the Bible is Revelation 21-22. These two chapters give a symbolic picture of the overwhelming beauty of heaven — a picture that illustrates the abundant provision of a loving heavenly Father. You have done nothing to merit such a reward. God chooses to give it to you. Equate this to earthly parents who want to do more than provide their children with bare essentials. Most parents instinctively want the very best for their children. What person can refuse such an outpouring of love by a Heavenly Father?

To be reminded of God's love gives you sound reason for self-esteem. You are valued by the Almighty. Your level of self-image is in direct proportion to your acceptance of this love.

Using Your Self-Image to Build a Better Marriage

It is not enough merely to know the facts about God's love and your consequent value. Before they serve any purpose, the facts need to be acted on. Knowing and doing go hand in hand. You may know how to drive a car, but if you never get behind the wheel, your knowledge is empty.

Many couples involved in a push-pull marriage know about

God's love for them, but they don't live in that love. As a result they go round and round in a push-pull pattern. Accumulated facts about self-image are not enough. Knowledge needs to be accompanied by appropriate behavior patterns.

Case Study: Putting Knowledge to Work

Rich and Donna had both grown up with a good "head knowledge" of God's love. They were married in a beautiful church and the ceremony included all the "right" words of Scripture. Throughout their adult lives, they attended church. Their children were in Bible study classes. You could say that Rich and Donna were a model church-going Christian couple.

But at home, Rich and Donna didn't always feel very Christian. It was common for them to needle each other with petty bickering. Donna usually operated from the puller's position by continually trying to get Rich to talk about her feelings on a given subject. Rich was the pusher, constantly working to avoid Donna's pleading. They argued frequently, and admitted they were easily discouraged and disappointed in their marriage.

At the peak of one of their bad times, Rich began questioning: "Why do I always feel down? Why can't I just be the husband I want to be?" He soon began to realize he wasn't making much effort to live in God's love. He was worried more about Donna's opinion than God's. As he shared his insight with Donna, something clicked. Donna recognized that she, too, had not been living in the light of God's love. She, too, had allowed her mate to determine her inner feelings of worth.

They both began to understand that if they didn't continually focus on the worthiness of their position with God, their reinforcement needs would automatically "drain" the other spouse. Because neither of them had the capacity to be all things to their mate, they would be in a no-win situation. Both decided to draw their strength first from God. He would be the one to give them a feeling of security and contentment. In doing so, they would be more capable of giving love since their individual "neediness" would be diminished. They knew these facts all their lives. But an uncomfortable marriage prompted them to put their knowledge of God's love to work.

To make the love of God the key factor in building your self-image, one attitude in particular helps: "I will not be threatened by my spouse's weaknesses." Put your trust in God. Be assured

God will never let you become involved in a circumstance without the strength to handle it (read I Cor. 10:13).

By taking the nonthreatened attitude, you are placing confidence in God and yourself. You can be confident—even in the middle of a trying situation—that you can get through it, not somehow, but triumphantly. Not only will you get through your struggles, you also have God's promise that your difficulties will result in your overall good (Rom. 8:28).

On a practical level, this means if your spouse has a bad temper, you don't lose heart. If your spouse nags constantly you know you can handle it. If your spouse is distant, rest easy in the confidence that all is not lost. In any case, focus first on the truth that your security rests in God's love. You can then commit yourself to claim that love in such a way that it becomes the overwhelming focus on your mind. Then finally, you can pray seeking God's will to learn the best way to respond in your moments of difficulty. When you claim the love of God more fully, you also claim the strength to work through the problems before you!

16

Commitment:
The Deciding Factor

We have covered a lot of information in this book. We have looked at ways to spot push-pull patterns in marriage. And we have contrasted these patterns with the factors involved in a give-and-take marriage. We have examined how a meaningful marital relationship can be established by sticking closely to God's design.

Now let's go back and underscore the point made in the Introduction: many people are able to accumulate information about good marriages and yet fail to have a good marriage. Their knowledge is not translated into action—at least not consistent action. To insure success in putting your information to good use, examine one final factor: commitment.

A marriage commitment is a private pledge you make publicly, and the extent of your commitment to each other determines the lengths you will go to in making your marriage a success. Your marriage commitment is also, in essence, an extension of your commitment to God. In marriage, the level of commitment is the most powerful factor in determining the ultimate success or failure of a partnership. With commitment you can combat seemingly insurmountable odds. Without it, you can't predict what will happen from one day to the next. Even through a host of ups and downs, you can win in marriage by determining that nothing will shake you from your initial pledge to your mate.

Some things in life require a great deal of personal planning and effort. For example, when you invite some couples over for dinner, you know you will have to work to prepare it. An athlete preparing for the big game knows that training and strategy sessions are part of the readiness process. An actor knows that behind every standing ovation is a script that had to be rehearsed over and over. Likewise, marriage partners can expect the best results when they make plans for commitment, expecting that persistence is vital to achieve the final goal of genuine intimacy.

Consider some key steps leading to the level of commitment needed for a solid marriage. These guidelines are not magic wands, but tools that require consistent use.

1. Develop loyalty toward your mate. When most people get married, their wedding vows include the words *for better or for worse*. But current divorce rates tell another story. People are committed for better, but not for worse. Most spouses will stand by one another when things go smoothly. But when times get rough, some want to run away. They are committed only in "fair weather."

Loyalty implies a sense of allegiance and dedication. This means that when stormy times arise, there are no "ifs" and "buts." With loyalty there is not so much a feeling of obligation as there is a sense of faithfulness and reliability. Loyal marriage partners recognize the sanctity of marriage. They don't feel so much like they have to stick it out; they want to. Their relationship means too much to take it lightly. When failures come, the automatic response is to look for ways to improve. True loyalty is not something that comes and goes. It exists in both the best of times and the most difficult of times.

2. Constantly be on the lookout for areas of self-improvement. The information contained in this book is for one purpose: to help you become a better mate. You will always have room for improvement. Look at this as an opportunity! You will be in an ongoing process of self-examination to find ways to refine your marriage skills.

A proper level of humility will be helpful (not in the sense of self-deprecation). Instead of being defensive about your shortcomings, you can be honest enough to pinpoint areas needing attention. So go ahead and admit it! When one mate seeks out areas of personal betterment, the marriage and family collectively reap the benefits.

3. Look for ways to verbalize your commitments. Commitments take on an entirely different dimension when they are expressed openly. As opposed to silent commitments, the spoken commitment is powerful. When you declare your intentions to your mate, the intentions will definitely become more genuine. Your commitments will come alive! You will feel a deeper sense of responsibility to follow through in your intentions.

What are some of the commitments that need to be openly expressed? First, there is the need to regularly remind your spouse of your love. "I love you" can go a long way in keeping a relationship healthy. But let's go a step further. After you tell your spouse of your love, openly explain how you plan to show your love. For example, you can say "I love you, and tonight instead of watching television I'd like to spend my time with you." Move love from a feeling to an action.

Beside proclaiming your love, you can verbalize your commitments in other ways. Tell your mate, for example, that you are in the process of learning to control your temper. You can let it be known that you are going to work at being a more understanding mate. You can tell your spouse that you are praying daily for a successful marriage. Each time you make your commitments known you are putting yourself on the line. This makes you more likely to follow through with your plans.

4. Join with other couples who have the same goals. Whether or not we want to admit it most of us are easily influenced by the people with whom we spend time. Consequently, when you join with other couples whose goal is to make their marriages work, you can be bouyed. From being with others who are committed to marriage, you can draw a sense of strength and encouragement. In turn, you can become a source of strength for them!

The most obvious place to find such a group of people is in a local, Bible-believing church. This is not to say that you will find perfect people there. But most members will hold the common goal of maturing in their Christianity. The value of joining with such a group is the team spirit that usually results. There is a desire to build up one another. You will grow in both Bible knowledge and in Christian fellowship. The company you keep is vital to the depth of your commitments.

5. Hold on to hope. Christians can cling to one specific promise that will carry them over any hurdle thrown in the path of marriage relationships. That is, there is no trial or temptation that can come on us in which God will not also provide the strength to overcome (read I Cor. 10:13). This means that if you are now trudging along in a difficult relationship, you can make improvements. There is hope!

By holding on tightly to hope, you are paying yourself a compliment. You are reinforcing the idea that you have the strength to carry through on the task set before you. You are claiming your worth as a person. You know that you have what it takes.

Hope will fuel your fire even when it is ready to die out. Marriage is an institution designed by God, and He is always there to give you guidance. Your challenge is to make yourself available to Him so that His will can be accomplished in your marriage. You will succeed when your commitment is so powerful that it causes you to turn your knowledge into action.